Helping Troubled Pupils

Helping Troubled Pupils

Chris Kyriacou

Nelson Thornes
a Wolters Kluwer business

Published in 2003 by:
Nelson Thornes Ltd
Delta Place
27 Bath Road
CHELTENHAM
GL53 7TH
United Kingdom

07 08 09 / 10 9 8 7 6 5 4

A catalogue record for this book is available from the British Library

ISBN 978 0 7487 7279 7

Typeset by Acorn Bookwork, Salisbury, Wiltshire
Printed and bound in Spain by GraphyCems

Contents

Introduction

During their school years, pupils will face a variety of personal problems. Sometimes these are severe and traumatic. This book focuses on some of the adverse circumstances that can give rise to major problems. The aim of the book is to consider how pupils may react in these circumstances and the role schools can play in helping pupils to deal with these circumstances.

The emphasis in this book is on understanding the nature of the adverse circumstances being considered and the role that teachers and schools can play, both within and outside the classroom, in helping pupils to cope with the circumstances they find themselves in. The book will also consider how teachers and schools can help pupils beforehand, either by making the situation less likely to occur or by giving pupils the knowledge and skills that will help them to cope if and when such a situation does occur.

Some ground rules

This book considers the type of general counselling that most teachers can be expected to give to pupils in schools. This normally takes the form of displaying empathy with the pupil and helping them to deal with the circumstances that confront them. Some pupils, however, may require therapeutic counselling to deal with a state of acute psychological disturbance, which requires professional intervention. The vast majority of teachers have not received specialist training in general counselling, and very few teachers will have been trained in therapeutic counselling. As a teacher you must know your limits, and be careful not to stray beyond your areas of competence.

There are three things we can expect of a teacher:

- to be able to identify a cause for concern
- to be able to give a pupil helpful advice and guidance on how to deal with the circumstances that confront them
- to be able to refer the cause for concern, if and when appropriate, to the member of staff with the appropriate expertise to deal with the case, who may then in turn consider how best to involve parents and outside agencies.

Dealing with a pupil in these circumstances may also have a powerful effect on you, and you need to be aware of your own personal vulnerabilities in deciding whether and how you wish to be involved in certain types of cases.

The adverse circumstances

The seven adverse circumstances chosen for consideration in this book cover the major areas of concern that most teachers will come across and will have to deal with at some point in their school careers. These are:

- bullying
- truancy
- exclusion
- stress
- abuse
- bereavement
- delinquency.

The impact of these adverse circumstances on pupils will vary immensely, depending on the age of the pupil, their personality, and the severity of the circumstances. The frequency of their occurrence will also vary immensely, and often there will be pupils who will experience these circumstances without teachers being aware of it.

Even if you are not involved directly in dealing with a particular case, you are very likely to be involved indirectly, as part of the school's more general policy of monitoring, helping and supporting pupils in distress. In addition, you may be involved in teaching parts of the school's personal, social and health education (PSHE) programme that is designed to help increase pupils' awareness of the adverse circumstances they may have to confront in their lives, and to help them develop skills that will help them to cope effectively.

Intended outcomes

By the end of this book, you should have gained an understanding of:

- the nature of the seven adverse circumstances listed above
- the psychological processes involved in pupils' reactions to these circumstances
- the organisational procedures in schools adopted to deal with these circumstances
- the role teachers can play in helping and supporting pupils in distress
- the role the school's PSHE programme can play in helping pupils to deal with these circumstances.

Readership

All teachers from time to time will be involved in helping pupils to deal with the adverse circumstances they find themselves in. The audience for this book comprises all those involved in supporting pupils, and provides appropriate guidance and material for teachers in initial training, teachers in the early part of their careers, and experienced teachers.

2 Helping

Pupils today face a huge range of problems and experiences which may give rise to distress, and schools can play a part in helping them to deal with the circumstances in which they find themselves (McNamara, 2000; Nicolson and Ayres, 1997). The impact that the adverse circumstances considered in this book will have on pupils will vary immensely from pupil to pupil. This impact will depend on the age of the pupil, their personality, the degree of support available, and the severity of the circumstances. Some pupils may appear to cope successfully with a minimum of distress. For others, the circumstances may result in severe and prolonged symptoms and mental health problems (Atkinson and Hornby, 2002). Between these two extremes, there are a great mass of cases where it is genuinely hard to tell how well the pupil is coping and what degree of help and support is needed.

Typical reactions indicating distress

There are many types of indicators that a pupil may be in distress. The most noteworthy indicators of these in school are:

- hostility
- detachment
- lack of interest
- violent outbursts
- muscle pains
- a worried look
- inability to concentrate
- becoming easily upset.

However, what is often quite crucial is noticing that there is a marked change in a pupil's behaviour which seems to be uncharacteristic of them and which, in itself, might not otherwise be regarded as a problem. For example, an attentive pupil who seems to find it difficult to concentrate, a cheerful pupil who becomes withdrawn, a diligent pupil whose work becomes cursory, may all indicate a possible problem occurring in their lives.

Some circumstances may be well known to many teachers in the school, such as persistent truancy. Some circumstances may only become known to the school following a contact from a parent or an outside agency, such as a bereavement. Some circumstances may never become known to the school, such as child abuse. Teachers therefore need to be vigilant, and at times proactive, in considering whether there is a cause for concern that requires investigating.

Defence mechanisms

Many reactions to adverse circumstances can be understood as mental defence mechanisms which distance the person mentally from the circumstances which would otherwise generate pain and anguish. The most common example of such a defence mechanism is denial, whereby the pupil either simply refuses to believe that the potentially stress-inducing events have in fact occurred, or accepts that they have occurred but simply claims that they are unimportant. An example would be a pupil who is bullied, who either denies, for example, that they were punched and kicked (e.g. 'Someone did bump into me but I don't remember being hit') or who interprets the event as of no consequence (e.g. 'It doesn't bother me if someone hits me sometimes, it's just one of those things'). In both cases of denial, it is important to realise that the pupil is not lying. Rather the pupil is mentally interpreting what has happened in a way that creates a memory that they can live with. This does, however, require mental energy, so whilst at a conscious level the pupil may be able to deny that they are being bullied, they will nevertheless still display other signs of distress, such as sleeplessness and looking worried. Another example of denial is the 'sour grapes' attitude, such as when a pupil who has been excluded or is at risk of being excluded claims 'I don't want to go to school anyway.'

Another reaction to adverse circumstances is disengagement. In life we often strive to reach important goals and this involves an investment of time and effort. As soon as it becomes apparent that the goal is not realistically achievable, a person will withdraw their effort. At the same time, they may switch their focus onto other goals that they feel might be achievable instead. Such disengagement avoids the anguish and pain that would accrue from striving for a goal that one simply will not achieve. By disengaging early, the sense of failure, when it eventually comes, will be reduced, as by then one is mentally focused on other goals. Disengagement is sometimes coupled with denial, since the person is in effect reducing in their own mind the importance of the original goal or exaggerating the importance of the new goals. For example, if a pupil who works hard at mathematics realises that they are not going to pass the GCSE, they may simply stop trying to do the work. They may claim that mathematics is unimportant to them. They may then start to claim that what really matters to them is to do well in sports activities or to leave school and get a job.

It is important to think about denial and disengagement in such a situation because they are not only symptoms of distress, but can also give misleading signals to teachers about the pupil's feelings, and may mask the hidden turmoil that is occurring which is not visible to the teacher. A pupil who stops doing their mathematics homework may not be challenging authority, but rather trying to protect their self-esteem. When a pupil says 'What's the point of doing this work?' it may really be meant as a genuine question rather than as intentional disobedience.

Continuing to strive for a goal that you know you will fail simply does not make sense to the pupil.

All teachers thus need to be aware that almost any set of adverse circumstances that typically generates a high level of stress can lead to pupils using denial and disengagement as part of their coping strategies. For example, following a bereavement a pupil may become totally engrossed in their school work or in some hobby. It may appear that the pupil seems to be completely unaffected by the bereavement. However, it is only by staying focused, almost obsessively, on some other aspect of their life, that they can disengage themselves from the family context and from thinking about the consequences for them of the bereavement.

Less serious and more serious cases

This book is primarily concerned with helping those pupils who, in adverse circumstances, require the support of teachers to overcome the distress they are experiencing. However, it is important to note the line that separates the less serious cases from the more serious cases.

Less serious cases are defined here as those pupils who exhibit signs of distress which can be addressed with little or no involvement of outside agencies (e.g. educational services, health services, social services and the voluntary sector). For these pupils, the support offered by those around them (parents, other relatives, friends and teachers) is sufficient to enable them to cope effectively with the adverse circumstances they face.

More serious cases are defined here as those pupils who develop *serious mental health problems*, which require the extended involvement of health care professionals. Some pupils with serious mental health problems may develop clinically diagnosed disorders. The two most common types of serious mental health disorder that may develop as a result of adverse circumstances are an *emotional disorder* and a *behavioural disorder*.

An emotional disorder most commonly involves anxiety, withdrawal and depression. Acts of self-harm (including attempts at suicide), serious drug abuse, and eating disorders such as anorexia and bulimia, are signs of major emotional problems. A behavioural disorder most commonly involves extreme aggression towards others and the persistent violation of rules. Such mental heath disorders can be precipitated by adverse circumstances when the circumstances have been severe and prolonged, such as in the case of sexual abuse that has been occurring for many years and that the pupil has been keeping a secret.

When the onset of the adverse circumstances is sudden and dramatic, this may result in an emotional disorder termed *post-traumatic stress disorder* (PTSD), characterised by pupils appearing to be in a continuous state of shock, having frequent and distressing thoughts about the event, sleeplessness and nightmares, inability to concentrate, and either being hyper-vigilant and easily startled or being emotionally withdrawn and detached. This disorder will be diagnosed at the point where it is judged that the symptoms seriously undermine the pupil's ability to lead a normal life and cope with everyday demands in a normal way (Atkinson and Hornby, 2002; Kinchin and Brown, 2001). PTSD is normally associated with the occurrence of disasters affecting a group of pupils, such as witnessing friends dying when a school coach is involved in an accident, or when a gunman walks into a school and starts shooting at pupils. However, the sudden onset of personal events can be also be traumatising, such as the sudden and unexpected death of a parent, or the onset of violent sexual abuse.

A survey by the Office for National Statistics (Meltzer *et al.*, 2000) of mental health problems in childhood and adolescence was based on data concerning 10,438 pupils aged 5 to 15 years. These included questionnaires completed by the parents, by the pupils themselves (for those aged 11 to 15 years) and by their teachers. The data on each pupil therefore comprised up to three sources. Meltzer *et al.* reported that 4 per cent of the pupils had an emotional disorder (including generalised anxiety disorder, depression, phobias and PTSD) and 6 per cent had a behavioural disorder (including conduct disorder, oppositional defiant disorder and attention deficit hyperactivity disorder). This figure of about 10 per cent of pupils having a mental disorder is in line with most estimates. This percentage tends to be higher for pupils who live in inner city areas, who are older, whose parents are unemployed, or who have special educational needs.

There are two main reasons why pupils who have special educational needs are relatively more vulnerable to such mental health disorders. Firstly, certain problems that give rise to their special educational needs (e.g. hearing problems, autism) may already generate a degree of stress which adverse circumstances (e.g. sexual abuse, bereavement) simply compound. Secondly, such problems may limit and impair their ability to develop effective coping strategies to deal with adverse circumstances (e.g. they may find it more difficult to explain their needs or worries to an adult).

Whilst a line can be drawn between less serious and more serious cases, at least in principle, it is important to recognise that, in practice, not all the more serious cases actually result in a referral to and the involvement of outside agencies. This is particularly the case for pupils who truant, and for pupils whose parents wish to distance themselves from the involvement of outside agencies. In both cases, the degree of mental health problems being experienced may, for these practical reasons, be difficult to assess. In addition, emotional problems (such as being very withdrawn) are more likely to be overlooked or accommodated because they usually cause less disruption to parents and teachers compared with behavioural problems. Meltzer *et al.* noted that 29 per cent of the pupils who had a mental disorder had not been seen by a health care specialist (such as a GP, paediatrician, social worker or educational psychologist) for help with their mental health problems.

How can schools help?

There are four approaches that schools can adopt in helping troubled pupils. The first approach is *empathetic*. This approach involves offering a supportive and empathetic climate to pupils in distress, and taking whatever action they can to ease the burden on pupils during their time of need. This approach may include general counselling, or it may simply involve taking action behind the scenes following consultation with parents or outside agencies. An example here would be sympathising with a pupil whose parent has just died.

The second approach is *problem-focused*. This involves action that a school can take to deal with the circumstances in a way that resolves the problems. An example here would be dealing with a case of bullying, which could focus on both helping the bully to understand that such behaviour is unacceptable and helping the victim to develop skills and strategies that would enable them to avoid becoming a target of a bully in the future.

The third approach is *educational*. This involves ensuring that the school's programme of PSHE includes elements that will help prepare pupils in some way for distressing circumstances they may have to face in their lives. An example of this would be education about coping skills, which can help prepare pupils to deal with examination pressures.

Finally, the fourth approach is *organisational*. This involves looking at the way in which school policies and practices can help minimise problems occurring in the first place. An example of this would be combating truancy by putting procedures into place which encourage good attendance, minimise pupil disaffection, and target with effective action those pupils whose attendance is giving cause for concern at an early stage.

Some circumstances may be dealt with by using a combination of all four approaches, whilst other circumstances will be addressed by only two or three of these approaches. In addition, the approaches used will vary from school to school, and also between pupils within the same school. For example, a school which serves a catchment where rates of juvenile delinquency are high is likely to have in place well-established elements in its PSHE programme dealing with promoting moral behaviour, and to have procedures to support pupils in avoiding criminal activity. Similarly, a school's approach to dealing with a bully who has a persistent record of bullying will be quite different from how it deals with a bully whose behaviour seems to be out of character.

Constraints on helping

A number of writers have pointed out some of the difficulties and problems facing schools in trying to support pupils experiencing distress. For example, a study by Nelson and While (2002) interviewed headteachers in 35 primary schools and heads of pastoral care in 46 secondary schools concerning the pastoral issues involved when caring for distressed pupils at school. The main constraints reported included the pressure on teachers to cope with the academic demands of the National Curriculum, which left inadequate time to devote to pastoral work; problems concerning the lack of privacy in the school, whereby a teacher and pupil could not easily find a place to talk undisturbed; problems of confidentiality, which meant that pupils were reluctant to disclose problems to a teacher if they felt these could be reported to a third party; teachers' worries about being alone with a pupil who was in distress and how to support and comfort them; and teachers feeling that they had not been trained in pastoral work. Nelson and While identify five essential elements needed for the effective pastoral care of distressed pupils:

- school environment: a caring and secure ethos
- responsive teachers: willing to listen and respond to pupils and parents
- collaboration: interprofessional and emergency support from outside agencies
- training: appropriate pastoral in-service training for all teachers
- supportive parents: responsive to all channels of communication.

The role of counselling

As stated in the introduction, this book is not concerned with therapeutic counselling, but rather with the type of general counselling that teachers can be expected to provide for pupils who are having problems but who are considered, with appropriate help and support, to be able to attend school and to cope reasonably well with the academic and social demands being made upon them (Lines, 2002; Long and Fogell, 1999; McGuiness, 1998; Sharp and Cowie, 1998). It may, of course, become clear that for some of these pupils general counselling on its own is not sufficient; other approaches and outside agencies may need to be involved and medical attention and therapeutic counselling may be required if the problems are to be addressed.

The stages of counselling

In counselling a pupil who is having problems there are a number of strategies and skills involved. The main purpose of counselling is to help the pupil. This involves three main elements:

- to help pupils to better understand the circumstances they find themselves in
- to help pupils to consider how they are reacting to these circumstances
- to help pupils to think about what would be helpful in improving their situation.

To achieve these objectives the teacher needs to structure their counselling into three main stages:

- to *listen* carefully to the pupil in order to explore the nature of the circumstances and the problems that the pupil is experiencing
- to *investigate* the circumstances further by consulting with others to get a fuller picture of what is happening
- to *propose action* that will help the pupil.

The above three stages can best be thought of as cyclic, so that in many cases one goes through the same three stages more than once before the process comes to a conclusion, as shown in Figure 2.1.

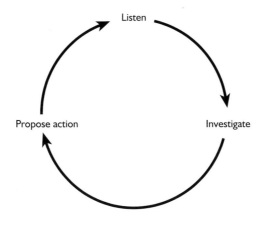

Figure 2.1 The counselling cycle

The first stage, listening, is crucial to good counselling. Listening carefully is difficult. In normal everyday conversation we do not really listen properly. Rather, we tend to just get the gist of what we are being told whilst we start to think ahead and formulate what we are going to say when it is our turn to speak. Listening in a counselling context requires very careful attention to what the pupil says, and the use of prompts to help the pupil further develop what they wish to say. The purpose of listening is to get as clear a picture as possible of the pupil's thoughts, feelings and needs. In this stage, the pupil should be doing most of the talking. Listening is best done somewhere quiet and where you can avoid being interrupted.

The next stage is to investigate the nature of the circumstances. Pupils may intentionally or unintentionally only give you part of the picture. Others involved may be able to provide further key information that provides a different perspective on what might lie at the heart of the problem. At this stage it may be important to involve outside agencies, particularly if a home visit may be important. Be very careful not to jump to conclusions. It is amazing how often when you hear one person's side of the story, you can feel absolutely confident that nothing can acceptably explain the actions of the other persons involved. However, when you hear what others have to say, you can often find that some critical aspects of the context or the sequence of events will lead you to interpreting what has happened very differently. Investigating therefore always needs to be conducted calmly and with an open mind.

The third stage is to propose action. The pupil should propose actions they feel would be helpful. Where the teacher proposes action they feel the school could take, this clearly needs to be negotiated with the pupil. In certain circumstances the pupil may wish to veto the action that the teacher proposes. However, in some circumstances there may be actions that you need to take that the pupil may feel unhappy about, but which you feel are in the pupil's interests, or which you are simply required to follow in accordance with school policy and legal responsibilities.

The counselling relationship

The counselling relationship between a teacher and a pupil is also very important. The pupil must feel trust towards the teacher, and the teacher needs to be supportive and to display empathy towards the pupil, in sympathising and understanding the problem the pupil is experiencing. Because the pupil's normal interaction with a teacher is in the classroom context of being taught and, where appropriate, being disciplined by the teacher, the pupil will normally view the teacher as an authority figure who is primarily there to promote pupils' learning and to keep them in order. The pastoral care aspect of a teacher's role thus needs to be signalled to the pupil in some way. This is normally achieved in secondary schools by means of form tutors and heads of pastoral care (such as a head of year or house), who make pupils aware that some teachers have a pastoral care role towards them. In primary schools, this formal pastoral care function is often accorded to the headteacher or a deputy headteacher. In many cases, however, it will be the normal classroom teacher who may initially need to deal with the circumstances facing the pupil. It is here that a softer tone of voice, listening skills and empathy can play a key part in helping the pupil to talk about their problems.

Counselling skills

McLaughlin (1995) has highlighted seven key counselling skills:

- the skills of attending and listening actively, which include the ability to paraphrase, summarise and reflect back
- the skills of appropriate questioning
- the ability to communicate empathetic understanding, non-critical acceptance and genuineness
- the ability to challenge
- the ability to share feelings and experiences in an appropriate way
- the ability to help the pupil set goals
- the ability to help the pupil solve problems and take appropriate action.

It is important, however, to emphasise again the distinction between the general counselling, support and empathy that teachers can be expected to show towards pupils who are having problems, and the therapeutic counselling that needs to be given by trained specialists.

Good practice in counselling support for pupils in schools is characterised by:

- school policies on key problem areas
- easy access to teachers who are approachable and can make time to listen to pupils.
- an integrated approach, which links the school's PSHE programme with pastoral work
- clear roles for both classroom teachers and those with designated pastoral care responsibilities

- good relationships with parents and outside agencies
- a careful match of counselling support to pupils' needs and perceptions.

Making sense of a pupil's reaction

In considering how a pupil is reacting to the problems and circumstances they are facing, we need to consider carefully whether their response may be a cause for concern. In doing this we need to distinguish whether the pupil is responding 'normally' or whether the pupil is behaving in a way that suggests something dysfunctional is occurring.

An important part of this involves considering the pupil's *mental representation of the social world*. This representation has two aspects to it. Firstly, the pupil's *self-identity*, which refers to how the pupil views their own key traits or characteristics as a person (e.g. kind, clever, bad at sports, tall, friendly). Secondly, their view of *social relationships*, which refers to how the pupil views their dealings with others (Can you trust other people? Do most new people you meet come to like you? Will adults help you if you have a problem?).

As children grow up, they develop their own unique mental representation of the social world that is shaped by their experiences. Most children will develop a normal and healthy representation, which will contain certain ideas, values, beliefs and expectations that are fairly typical of all individuals in the society and culture to which they belong. Aspects of these will also be influenced by their membership of particular subcultures within their society, such as membership of a particular ethnic group, religion or locality.

If, for example, a pupil responds to a bereavement by feeling sad, or to news of failing an important test by behaving in an aggressive way towards their friends, these are in effect expressions of an underlying normal reaction to their situation. Even if their reaction becomes more noticeable, such as crying continuously during the lunch break, that can still be regarded as being within the bounds of normality, although the more excessive and inappropriate the behaviour becomes, the greater will be the cause for concern generated.

If, however, a pupil responds by becoming paranoid and interpreting everyone else's behaviour as being hostile towards them, this would suggest that the circumstances have deeply affected their view of the social world around them and the way they now interpret their social relationships with others. This is not simply a case of an extreme version of a normal response to adverse circumstances. Rather, the pupil's mental representation of themselves (their self-identity) and how they relate to those around them (their view of social relationships) has become 'pathological'. Such cases are more likely to occur in response to prolonged adverse circumstances than they are in response to one-off events, such as prolonged sexual abuse. In these cases, the pupil is only able to adapt and cope with the circumstances by developing a self-protective view of their self-identity and the world around them, which will enable them to make sense of what is happening to them. If such sexual abuse starts to occur at a relatively late age, at about 12 or 13 years, the pupil is likely to have developed before then a reasonably healthy and normal representation of the social world, so that when the abuse begins, it has the effect of altering what was until then a healthy and normal representation. However, if the abuse starts at a much younger age, say at about 3 or 4 years, the child's mental representation of themselves and how they relate socially to others around them may not yet have had a chance to develop and mature normally. The earlier such abuse starts, the more likely it is that the pupil's representation of the social world will have pathological elements within it which may become very resistant to change later in life, even after extensive therapy.

As a teacher dealing with a pupil who is giving cause for concern, you need to be very careful not to make assumptions about how and why a pupil's behaviour may be abnormal or unacceptable or inappropriate. In some cases, the response displayed by a pupil will be an expression of problems and traumas that occurred much earlier in their lives and are being reawakened by the circumstances they are now confronted with. In addition, the distinction between having a healthy mental representation of the social world and having a pathological one is not always clear. All of us have elements of our mental representation that might be deemed unhealthy, abnormal or even pathological. These may only be revealed in extreme situations, which will differ from person to person. For example, one person might find that they react very badly to a situation in which they think they have been let down by someone they trusted. Another person might be extremely upset by being passed over for a promotion. We often do not fully understand why we sometimes feel such strong negative reactions to certain types of situations, and on some occasions the intensity of our feelings can take us by surprise.

The role of the teacher is not to act as a therapist. Rather it is to be sensitive to signs that a pupil is in distress and to provide support. If the cause for concern continues, that is the time to explore the options for extending the support, which may need to involve professional counselling and psychiatric help.

In such cases, the counsellor will need to consider whether the disturbing behaviour is primarily an expression of an excessive reaction in a pupil whose mental representation of the social world is in essence normal and healthy, or whether it is an expression of a mental representation that is or has become pathological in some way. This has major implications for the type of therapeutic intervention that needs to be undertaken and its chance of success.

A full understanding of the way in which pupils respond to the seven adverse circumstances that are addressed in this book thus needs to take account of the pupil's mental representation of the social world. It is important to note, however, that this mental representation has both a cognitive dimension (knowledge) and an emotional dimension (feelings), and both dimensions will influence how the pupil responds to adversity.

For example, the feelings that follow a bereavement may include guilt, anger, revenge, jealousy and hopelessness. The emotions that come to the fore will in part be a reflection of a rational, normal and healthy response to the circumstances. For example, feeling angry and sad is a natural response to the loss of someone you love. One pupil might feel jealous of other pupils who still have both parents whilst they have lost a father or mother, and become very withdrawn. Another pupil might experience strong feelings of revenge because they feel society has in some way deliberately deprived them of a parent who they were fairly entitled to expect would be around for many years, and start bullying other pupils. These different reactions, in terms of both their feelings and their behaviour, to the same event will owe much to the cognitive and emotional history of their mental representation of the social world.

Pupils in counselling will often need help to come to understand why they may experience such strong negative emotions, and to recognise that these will in part be influenced by all the experiences they had whilst growing up. This will help them to realise that their current feelings are not simply something that they have intentionally generated and that can easily be switched off with sufficient will-power, but rather that these emotions reflect their individual cognitive and emotional development, and that with appropriate counselling and/or with appropriate training in emotion control strategies, their inappropriate behaviour can be altered.

More serious cases of distress, where mental health problems are evident, will need to be treated by mental health professionals, who include therapeutic counsellors, clinical psychologists and psychiatrists. Whilst pupils are receiving such treatment, they usually continue to attend school, where they will need the help and support of teachers.

Encourage the pupil to talk

When counselling pupils, ask questions that encourage the pupil to talk. This can be done by avoiding questions that simply require yes or no answers. However, be careful not to pry unnecessarily into a pupil's personal life or to encourage the pupil to disclose something they may regret telling you about later. Counselling needs to be sensitive to a pupil's mood and wishes, and what a pupil tells you needs to be freely given.

Don't be afraid of silences

Do not feel you need to fill any silences that occur. Pupils need thinking time to reflect on their position and needs, and to prepare themselves to say something to you that is difficult to disclose. Silences and thinking time are crucial to helping pupils prepare what they want to say.

Ask a pupil what they would find helpful and supportive

Pupils' circumstances and needs vary greatly. Being supportive and helpful involves taking account of a pupil's personality and coping behaviour.

Asking a pupil what they would find helpful and supportive is often the best and most sensible way of tailoring what the school can offer to address the pupil's needs.

Don't encourage the pupil to show emotion

When pupils are facing difficult circumstances, it is quite natural for them to feel afraid and tearful. Indeed, there are many circumstances where it comes as no surprise to see a pupil cry, and you need to say that it's okay to cry. However, be careful not to regard crying as something you should encourage. For some pupils, not showing emotion is an important part of their coping strategy, and what they might most value is your helping them to stay calm and composed. If you think a pupil is about to start crying, you might ask them to blow their nose or you can change the subject. You should not assume that a person needs to show emotion or react in a way you would do. Nor is it your job to be an amateur therapist. Your job is primarily to be supportive and empathetic, and to consider how best the school can help a pupil during a period of distress.

Don't stray beyond your areas of competence

In talking to pupils about their circumstances, you may find yourself dealing with problems that are outside your areas of competence. In some cases, this will be immediately obvious to you, and you will need to refer the matter to a colleague. In contrast, there are some cases where you will feel confident about giving advice and support. In between these two extremes are cases where you will be unsure how best to proceed. When in any doubt, seek advice. It is neither in your interests nor in the pupil's interests for you to stray into areas of counselling where you simply do not have access to the information you need, an awareness of the school's policies and procedures for dealing with these circumstances, an awareness of the educational legislation, or the interpersonal skills to explore the situation skilfully.

Don't get personally involved

As a member of one of the helping professions, you will frequently be dealing with pupils facing acute and distressing problems, where you feel a personal intervention by you can make a real difference. It is often tempting to go beyond your role as a teacher, and to become personally involved in some way. You might feel you want to visit the pupils' parents in their home. You might feel some financial help will solve some of the problems. You might feel you need to follow a case through long after it has been referred to a colleague or an outside agency. It is very important to be aware of the limits of your role as teacher, and to recognise that you need to play your part in a wider system that is in place to offer appropriate help and support. There are three main reasons why you need to place a limit on your involvement in helping troubled pupils. Firstly, few cases are as simple as they may appear to be from your own view of the circumstances. Secondly, it is easy to act with the best of intentions in a way that can be counter-productive. Thirdly, it is simply not viable for you to get personally involved, given the costs on your time and emotional state that such involvement would demand.

Don't agree to keep secrets

From time to time you may be approached by a pupil who wishes to say something to you in confidence. They may explicitly ask whether they can tell you something that you must not reveal to anyone else. In these circumstances you might reply 'If you've got a problem I might be able to help with, please tell me what it is, but I can't promise not to tell anyone else if it's something very serious'. It is important not to agree to keep something secret. Some problems will require you to take action that involves informing others, and indeed you may be under a legal obligation to do so, such as in cases of child abuse. Similarly, teachers have no privilege of confidentially which is unimpeachable by law (Lines, 2002). However, quite apart from the legal issues involved, as a teacher you should not become involved in acquiring information that you agree not to pass on if the situation requires it.

Don't gossip

Teachers are, however, expected to maintain confidentiality. This means that access to sensitive information given to you by a pupil needs to be private, and should only be recorded and shared with others within the context of confidentiality. It is quite tempting to share information about pupils with colleagues as part of everyday social conversations of human interest. Indeed, much important information about pupils that colleagues need to be aware of is transmitted in a casual manner in the staffroom. However, you need to be aware of the line that has to be drawn between information that can be shared in this way and information that needs to be kept confidential.

Be aware of the effects of counselling on your own emotional state

It is also important to be aware of the emotional impact that counselling can have on you in dealing with sensitive issues. Hearing about cases of bullying, bereavement or abuse, for example, can be extremely upsetting. Be careful not to allow your own emotions to spill over into inappropriate actions. Moreover, you may find that in extreme cases you may require some counselling yourself to come to terms with the situation you have had to deal with.

References

Atkinson, M. and Hornby, G. (2002) *Mental Health Handbook for Schools.* London: RoutledgeFalmer.

Kinchin, D. and Brown, E. (2001) *Supporting Children with Post-traumatic Stress Disorder: A Practical Guide for Teachers and Professionals.* London: David Fulton.

Lines, D. (2002) *Brief Counselling in Schools.* London: Sage.

Long, R. and Fogell, J. (1999) *Supporting Pupils with Emotional Difficulties.* London: David Fulton.

McGuiness, J. (1998) *Counselling in Schools: New Perspectives.* London: Cassell.

McLaughlin, C. (1995) 'Counselling in schools: its place and purpose.' In R. Best, P. Lang, C. Lodge and C. Watkins (eds) *Pastoral Care and Personal-Social Education: Entitlement and Provision* (pp. 61–74). London: Cassell.

McNamara, S. (2000) *Stress in Young People: What's New and What Can We Do?* London: Continuum.

Meltzer, H., Gatward, R., Goodman, R. and Ford, T. (2000) *Mental Health of Children and Adolescents in Great Britain.* London: The Stationery Office.

Nelson, E. and While, D. (2002) 'Constraints to pastoral care for distressed children: opinions of head teachers.' *Pastoral Care in Education*, 20(3), 21–8.

Nicolson, D. and Ayres, H. (1997) *Adolescent Problems: A Practical Guide for Parents and Teachers.* London: David Fulton.

Sharp, S. and Cowie, H. (1998) *Counselling and Supporting Children in Distress.* London: Sage.

3 Bullying

Bullying in schools was for a long time accepted as just one of those things that occurs from time to time. However, in recent years research has indicated that it is much more widespread than many thought and that the damage it can do to victims can be very serious and have long-term effects. In some cases, pupils have been driven to suicide as a result of being bullied. The increased awareness of bullying has led to a number of major initiatives aimed at combating bullying in schools. All schools are now expected to have a clear policy and programme to deal with bullying, and a number of innovative schemes have been used to tackle this problem. Whilst bullying in schools will never be eradicated, there is little doubt that the concerted efforts now in place to deal with bullying are doing much to reduce its occurrence, and to offer help to both bullies and victims.

What do we mean by 'bullying' and how common is it?

Bullying can be defined as persistent aggressive behaviour by one pupil towards another, intended to cause the victim to suffer. The behaviour may be:

- *physical* (e.g. hitting, pushing)
- *verbal* (e.g. name calling, teasing)
- *indirect* (e.g. social exclusion, making gestures).

Bullying is targeted on the victim on several occasions. The bully may be acting alone or as part of a group. The bully normally has some sort of power over the victim, such as being stronger or acting in a group.

Studies of bullying reveal that it is a major concern in many schools throughout the world (Smith *et al.*, 1999b). Interestingly, many languages do not have a word for bullying, and often refer to the English word in their educational writings. Many countries simply subsume it under a general phrase referring to violence or aggression in school. However, to really understand bullying it is essential to make a distinction between one-off instances of violent and aggressive behaviour, and the prolonged and repeated victimisation that constitutes the heart of the bullying process.

The notion of intentionality is also important here. There are many instances where the pupil causing the distress claims that it was unintentional, that the occasional teasing and intimidation was simply part of the everyday rough and tumble of school life, and there was no intention to cause the victim prolonged distress. It is perfectly true that many cases of pupils reporting that they have been bullied can be traced back to a misunderstanding of this sort, and that the problem will go away as soon as the perpetrator is made aware of the distress that their behaviour has caused. In true cases of bullying, however, the bully is fully aware of the distress that is being caused, and it is the taking of pleasure in this distress that is the real reason why the bully maintains their focus on a victim. Nevertheless, unintended distress is just as upsetting as bullying and also needs to be dealt with effectively.

Following the seminal work by Olweus on bullying in Scandinavia in the 1970s, a large number of studies have been conducted looking at the nature and extent of bullying in schools (e.g. Olweus, 1993, 1996; Smith and Sharp, 1994; Smith *et al.*, 1999b).

The DfES (2002) notes that the emotional distress caused by bullying can lead to lower attainment, truancy and, in extreme cases, suicide. The DfES estimates that a third of all girls and a quarter of all boys are at some time afraid of going to school because of bullying.

Estimating the incidence of bullying

Establishing the incidence of bullying in schools is very difficult, since only a small proportion of cases is reported to teachers. Most of the estimates are thus based on self-report measures. For example, a study by Austin and Joseph (1996) of 425 primary school pupils in Merseyside aged 8 to 11 years using a self-report scale classified 9 per cent of the pupils as 'bullies only', 22 per cent as 'victims only', 15 per cent as 'both bullies and victims' and 54 per cent as 'neither bully nor victim'. A survey of 2623 pupils by Whitney and Smith (1993) in Sheffield found that 10 per cent of primary school pupils and 4 per cent of secondary school pupils reported being bullied 'at least once a week'.

In addition, what counts as bullying also varies. For example, Boulton (1997) explored the views of 138 primary and secondary teachers in the North West of England on what they regarded as bullying, by asking them to rate whether certain behaviours were viewed as bullying. Whereas 97 per cent agreed that 'threatening people verbally' was bullying, only 48 per cent agreed that 'leaving someone out' was. These differences indicate that when a teacher is faced with a report of a particular incident in school, in many cases it will not be easy to decide if it constituted bullying and that different teachers may sometimes come to different conclusions.

A study by Branwhite (1994) asked 836 Year 7 pupils aged 11 to 12 years to consider 14 items representing potential sources of social stress and to indicate whether they had experienced the relevant event and thought a lot about it afterwards. Forty-three per cent of the pupils responded 'yes' to the item 'being called names by a lot of other students' and 19 per cent to the item 'being pushed around, hit, or kicked a lot by other students'.

Exploring the incidence of bullying with young children is particularly problematic, as their notion of what constitutes bullying is not as precise as that of older children. For example, a study by Smith and Levan (1995) explored the definitions and experiences of bullying with 60 pupils aged 6 to 7 years using a pictorial questionnaire. They found that 14 per cent of the pupils reported that they had been bullied in the previous week, but also that many of the pupils appeared to regard general, one-off incidents of fighting and aggressive behaviour as bullying.

A study by Boulton and Underwood (1992) of 296 pupils in middle schools in Yorkshire aged 8 to 12 years also highlighted the extent of bullying that occurs on the journey to and from school (reported by 25 per cent of the pupils) and in the streets near where they live or in nearby parks and playing fields (reported by 32 per cent of the pupils).

Our best estimate is that about 20 per cent of pupils will have been the victim of serious bullying at some point in their school careers, ranging from persistent teasing and name calling at one extreme to physical attacks and extortion at the other extreme. Whilst the latter tends to be regarded as more serious, there have been many cases where persistent verbal abuse has led a pupil to commit suicide. The judgement of seriousness thus depends not just on the action but also on the effect it is having on the victim. For example, Weaver (2000) reports a case study of an adolescent girl who, after repeated emotional bullying at school, developed symptoms consistent with those of post-traumatic stress disorder. It appears therefore that in some cases repeated low-level bullying can precipitate a reaction on a par with a sudden traumatic event.

Why do some pupils become bullies and others victims?

Generalisations based on research on bullies and victims need to be treated with caution because the patterns can vary so much from school to school. In general, however, the following points can be made: both boys and girls may be bullies, but bullying is more common amongst boys; boys are equally likely to be acting alone or in a group, whilst girls are more likely to act as part of a group; bullies are more likely to be the same age as their victim rather than older; boys are more likely to use physical bullying, whilst girls use verbal or indirect bullying; bullying decreases steadily from the age of 8 to 16 years (Olweus, 1996; Smith *et al.*, 1999a, 1999b).

Bullies and victims

Bullies vary a great deal, but have a greater tendency than the average pupil to come from homes where discipline is inconsistent or excessive and where family relationships show little warmth, and to act aggressively towards others, including adults. However, many bullies are perfectly 'normal' and some writers have argued that there is a danger in demonising bullies as being different from other pupils and that most pupils, if the circumstances are appropriate, may become involved in bullying. The point is also often made that bullies may be victims too, not only of being bullied themselves, but of personal problems arising from their home circumstances, such as a parental bereavement, and it is worth noting that some bullies have psychiatric problems which require medical attention (Salmon *et al.*, 2000). It is also important to distinguish between those pupils who are persistent bullies and who take the lead in instigating bullying, and other pupils who simply join in the bullying which is instigated by these leaders. The former group are likely to comprise no more than 5 per cent of pupils, whereas a much larger group of pupils can be encouraged to join in once bullying is occurring. It is the former group that is particularly likely to suffer from problems in their home circumstances and to engage consistently in various types of anti-social behaviour during the school years. The main attraction of bullying is that it enhances the bully's self-image, which is likely to be particularly important for pupils who have a low self-esteem, and indeed there are some studies which indicate that bullies are perceived by some pupils as 'cool' (Pateraki and Houndoumadi, 2001).

Victims also vary a great deal, but have a greater tendency than the average pupil to come from an over-protective family environment, to lack friends at school, to be insecure, to act inappropriately in social settings, to react to bullying incidents submissively or by being upset, or to be seen as obviously different in some way in terms of appearance, ethnic origin, personality, ability or special educational needs. Given that a large proportion of pupils will be victims of bullying at some point during their school years, we need to understand why only some of these become consistent long-term victims of bullying whilst others do not. A crucial factor appears to be the way in which they respond to the initial bullying. Some pupils are able to use their social skills and common sense to avoid further bullying by learning to avoid those situations, behaviours and locations where the bullying is likely to continue. They also use coping strategies such as assertiveness and humour to deal effectively with the circumstances that give rise to bullying. Perhaps most importantly of all, the victims do not get upset and display distress. Bullying depends on a relationship being established between the bully and the victim in which the bully can take pleasure in the overt suffering that the victim displays. If the victim does not display such distress this relationship is broken. Some researchers have described the strategies used by pupils which are effective in dealing with being bullied as *resilient coping strategies* (e.g. use of humour, being assertive) and those which are likely to prolong the bullying as *vulnerable coping strategies* (e.g. getting upset, pleading to be left alone). It is for this reason that programmes which aim to help victims seek to improve their use of resilient coping strategies.

A study by Cullingford and Brown (1995) looked at the views of 128 primary school pupils aged 8 to 11 years regarding bullies and victims. Most pupils thought the main motive for bullies was the need to act tough and show off in front of others, although some noted that the bullies themselves might have problems or be insecure. Of particular interest are the views they gave as to why some pupils became victims. Although 30 per cent could not detect any clear reason, 36 per cent said that pupils became victims because they were 'different', for example in terms of their appearance or the way they behave. Cullingford and Brown make the point that once a difference has been found and a nickname applied, there seems to be a collective awareness that a victim has been identified.

Stuart and McCullagh (1996) explored the views of 400 primary school pupils in Northern Ireland regarding bullies and victims. They reported that the most frequent traits associated with bullies were 'show off', 'confident' and 'big', and the most frequent traits associated with victims were 'sad', 'obedient to parents' and 'weak'.

A study by Borg (1998) looked at the emotional reactions associated with bullying as reported by 3071 self-declared bullies and 3801 self-declared victims using a questionnaire survey of primary and secondary school pupils in Malta. Interestingly, about half of the bullies said they felt sorry after the incident. The dominant feeling for the victim was vengefulness and anger, but a substantial proportion of victims felt either self-pity, indifference or helplessness. Also of interest were the responses of the victims as to what they did after the incident. The highest proportion overall (31 per cent) said they did nothing, whilst 22 per cent said they sought the help of a teacher (although it is noteworthy that the proportion seeking the help of a teacher dropped from 33 per cent for primary school pupils to 16 per cent for secondary school pupils).

Long-term consequences

A number of studies have looked at the long-term consequences of bullying on victims' psychological adjustment and educational progress. Not only are victims of frequent and prolonged bullying made unhappy by being bullied, but they may also develop mental health problems, become truants or school refusers, do less well at school academically than they would otherwise have done, and in extreme cases be driven to commit suicide. Given the widespread occurrence of bullying, most pupils can claim to have been victims of it at some point in their school careers. However, it is frequent and prolonged bullying that is likely to have long-term consequences. For example, a study by Juvonen *et al.* (2000) focused on an ethnically diverse sample of 244 middle school pupils aged 12 to 15 years in Los Angeles, USA. Their measure of being bullied was based on the self-reported frequency of personally experienced incidents. Interestingly, the most frequently reported incident was 'rumours' (77 per cent reported that this had happened to them during the school year), followed by 'name calling' (66 per cent), 'public ridicule and humiliation' (66 per cent) and 'property theft and damage' (63 per cent). They reported that pupils who were frequently bullied were more likely to feel lonely, depressed and victimised, and to have a lower sense of self-worth, and that this in turn led to greater absenteeism from school and lower educational attainment.

A study by Roland (2002) looked at the incidence of depression and suicidal thoughts amongst bullies and victims, based on a sample of 2088 secondary school pupils in Norway aged 14 years. He reported that both bullies and victims had a much higher rate of depressive symptoms and suicidal thoughts compared with other pupils. Roland argues that the high level of depressive symptoms and suicidal thoughts in bullies probably stems from their family circumstances, where factors such as relationship problems, disharmony and aggression at home contribute both to their becoming a bully and to becoming depressed. In contrast, the high level of depression for victims probably stems directly from the act of being bullied itself.

A study by Crozier and Skliopidou (2002) looked at the recollections of an opportunity sample of 220 adults with regard to being called names at school. Sixty-four per cent of them recalled hurtful names, the most frequent of which fell into three categories: those based on their appearance (e.g. midget, freckles), a play on their name (e.g. Santa, Twang), and a reference to animals (whale, ferret). The most common form of response was 'retaliation', either verbal or physical, and the least frequent response was to tell the teacher. Amongst those who reported being extremely hurt or very hurt by the name calling, this name calling was associated with an earlier onset and longer experience of physical bullying, and also had a greater negative impact on their experience of school in terms of academic work, attendance, enjoyment of school, friendships and participation in activities. The study indicates that hurtful name calling may have a greater negative impact on pupils both in the short term and in the long term than has been commonly recognised, and the fact that it is less obvious to teachers may make this form of bullying particularly pernicious.

What can schools do to help the bully and the bullied, and to deal with bullying?

The DfES (2002) notes that a legal duty is placed on headteachers to draw up procedures to prevent bullying among pupils and to bring these procedures to the attention of staff, parents and pupils. Effective anti-bullying strategies should form part of a school's discipline and behaviour policy. Procedures for staff, parents and pupils to follow if bullying occurs should be clear and well publicised throughout the school. An extract from a school's policy document for staff on bullying is shown in Figure 3.1.

Figure 3.1 Guidance on bullying

A   AIMS
- To emphasise the issue for staff and remind them of their roles in preventing bullying.
- To seek parents' and Governors' endorsement of the school approach.
- To re-emphasise to children what the school's values are and how to act.
- To outline the school's broad interpretation of what constitutes bullying and the prompt, stern measures it takes when instances occur.

B   DEFINITION
- Any systematic physical, verbal, psychological or sexual intimidation – usually by those in a position of power against those unable to defend themselves.
- Implies wilful desire to hurt, threaten, frighten in order to cause distress.
- Implies personal gratification for the bully or desire to impress.
- It is possible for a child to be a bully unconsciously and without serious intent to hurt.

C   TYPES OF BULLYING
- Taunting, teasing, name calling, mocking physical or racial characteristics, shouting insults.
- Touching, poking, pointing, pushing, scuffling, barging, actual hitting, threatening violence.
- Malicious whispering to others, ganging up, 'Coventry', deliberately isolating, and group bullying.
- Hiding personal belongings, defacing work, rubbishing achievement.

D   LOCATION
- In the lightly supervised areas of school such as distant parts of the fields, in toilets, behind Youth Club, bike sheds
- On the corridors at breaks, lunches and change of lesson
- On the school buses
- Walking to and from school
- In the cloakrooms
- In classrooms, e.g. group work
- In the dining room

E   ACTION IN THE EVENT OF BULLYING
- Refer to Head of Year/Head of School/Involve Form Tutor
- Investigation – written statements
- Counsel victim and contact parents. Give support to victim. Suggest victim talks to a listener
- Choose level of punitive response appropriate for the bully and contact parents –
    - severe reprimand
    - detention
    - isolation
    - see parents
    - temporary exclusion
- Consider counselling/referral to Pupil Support Services so that the bully can understand her/his behaviour and its effect on others. Ensure the bully understands the consequences of repeating the offence and orchestrating others
- Monitor effectiveness of intervention
- Possibly use 'the shared concern approach'

Figure 3.1;   (contd)

Since the early 1990s, the literature aimed to help schools to reduce bullying has mushroomed (Guerin and Hennessy, 2002; Rigby, 2001; Sharp and Thompson, 2001). The DFE (1994) launched an anti-bullying pack in England and Wales, and SCRE (1992, 1993) did so in Scotland. These packs aimed to help schools to develop a whole-school policy, and include ideas and materials for teachers, non-teaching staff and parents.

The DFE pack, called *Don't Suffer in Silence*, includes the following information for pupils:

When you are being bullied

- Be firm and clear: look them in the eye and tell them to stop.
- Get away from the situation as quickly as possible.
- Tell an adult what has happened straight away.

After you have been bullied

- Tell a teacher or another adult in your school.
- Tell your family.
- If you are scared to tell a teacher or an adult on your own, ask a friend to go with you.
- Keep on speaking up until someone listens.
- Do not blame yourself for what has happened.

When you are talking about bullying with an adult, be clear about

- what has happened to you
- how often it has happened
- who was involved
- who saw what was happening
- where it happened
- what you have done about it already.

The DFE pack also contains advice for parents about how to stop their child from bullying others:

- Talk with your child; explain that what he/she is doing is unacceptable and makes other children unhappy.
- Discourage other members of your family from bullying behaviour or from using aggression or force to get what they want.
- Show your child how he/she can join in with other children without bullying.
- Make an appointment to see your child's teacher or form tutor; explain to the teacher the problems your child is experiencing; discuss with the teacher how you and the school can stop him/her bullying others.
- Regularly check with your child how things are going at school.

- Give your child lots of praise and encouragement when he/she is cooperative or kind to other people.

The DfES (2002) has also established a website for *Don't Suffer in Silence* which provides ideas and practical techniques for all those involved in combating bullying.

The first SCRE pack (1992) offered some ideas for teachers on what to do if you come across bullying in school:

First steps

- Remain calm: you are in charge; reacting emotionally may add to the bully's fun and give the bully control of the situation.
- Take the incident or report seriously.
- Take action as quickly as possible.
- Think hard about whether your action needs to be private or public: who are the pupils involved?
- Reassure the victim: do not make the victim feel inadequate or foolish.
- Offer concrete help, advice and support to the victim.
- Make it plain to the bully that you disapprove.
- Encourage the bully to see the victim's point of view.
- Punish the bully if you have to, but be very careful how you do this: reacting aggressively gives the message that it is all right to bully if you have the power.
- Explain clearly the punishment and why it is being given.

Involving others

- Inform school management and/or other appropriate persons, e.g. the guidance staff in secondary school, or the head of the infant department in a primary school.
- Inform colleagues if the incident arose in a situation where everyone should be vigilant, e.g. unsupervised toilets.
- Inform, or ask your headteacher to inform, both sets of parents calmly, clearly and concisely; reassure both sets of parents that the incident will not linger on or be held against anyone.

Final steps

- Make sure the incident does not live on through reminders from you.
- Try to think ahead to prevent a recurrence of the incident, if you uncover the trigger factor.

Don't

- be over-protective and refuse to allow the victim to help him/herself
- assume the bully is bad through and through: try to look objectively at the behaviour with the bully

- keep the whole incident from the parents of the victim or of the bully
- call in the parents without having a constructive plan to offer either side.

The second SCRE pack (1993) highlights three points that emerged from teachers', pupils' and parents' reports about tackling bullying which need to be emphasised, and provides an example which highlights for each of these the sorts of problems that can occur:

- *Take the incident or report seriously and be wary of 'labelling' pupils or parents.* For example, the father of an 11-year-old girl went to the school to complain that his son had been punched by a classmate and was told not to get things out of proportion and to consider that the bully had problems at home.
- *Offer concrete help, advice, support and feedback to the victims and their families.* For example, after a year of bullying, a father reported that his son finally informed the deputy head about being bullied and no action was taken.
- *Encourage the bully to see the victim's point of view.* For example, a teacher reported that getting the bully to empathise with the victim had led to an 'over the top' outpouring of suggested ways to make amends that were unlikely to happen.

These three examples illustrate how every case is complex, and ripe for poor communication and misunderstanding. In some cases a school thinks it has dealt successfully with the bullying, but neglects to inform the victim or the victim's parents about the action that has been taken. In other cases, the school is often not in a position to fully inform both parties (the bully or the victim) of what it knows or what action might have been taken 'behind the scenes', and on occasions it can be in the pupils' interests to be kept in ignorance. Whilst schools need to keep pupils and their families informed of how the bullying has been or is being resolved, this has to be done with sensitivity to the needs of the pupils concerned.

Victims' reluctance to report bullying

A number of studies have indicated that a major problem in tackling bullying is the reluctance of victims to report such incidents. A case study of bullying at one secondary school by Sewell (1999) identified eight common reasons why victims did not report bullying to teachers:

- a perception that the actions taken against them did not constitute bullying
- a sense of loyalty to the student community and that it would be betraying ('grassing on') their peers
- a fear of reprisal by the bully or other pupils
- a perception that society expects them to be able to look after themselves and the embarrassment of confessing to being a victim
- a perception that the bullying was their own fault
- an ability to cope with or tolerate the bullying
- a lack of opportunity to talk to a teacher

- a feeling that there was no obvious solution to the problem and therefore no one would be able to help them.

For these reasons, many anti-bullying programmes employ strategies in which the need for a victim to report bullying to a teacher plays only a small part.

School approaches to tackling bullying

A number of studies have been reported which have sought to evaluate the effectiveness of different types of intervention strategies. Almost all indicate that the development of a whole-school policy, an education programme for pupils highlighting the need to combat bullying, and the use of a mediation programme for bullies and victims, do have an effect on reducing bullying, but the effect is limited, and it is unlikely that schools will be able to reduce bullying to negligible levels. The effects of anti-bullying programmes seem to be more powerful in primary schools, possibly because in secondary schools we are dealing with a hard core of bullies who are more resistant to the effects of such programmes on their behaviour. Nevertheless, given the suffering that bullying causes, any action that markedly reduces such incidents has to be regarded as important.

For example, a study by Stevens *et al.* (2000) evaluated an anti-bullying programme in 18 primary and secondary schools in Belgium based on creating a more positive school atmosphere within which there were clear rules against unacceptable peer interactions. The programme involved activities at three levels: (1) for bullies and victims, (2) for pupils in general, and (3) for teachers, non-teaching staff and parents. The activities included manuals, videos, the development of an anti-bullying school policy, active learning activities for pupils to develop attitudes and skills to combat bullying, a social learning approach to dealing with bullies by helping them to understand the consequences of their actions, and emotional support and advice for victims. Whilst the study indicated a number of ways in which the intervention programme had been successful, it also highlighted the complex way in which different aspects of the programme can impact differently in different schools. It is clear that each school needs to tailor their intervention strategies to their particular needs and circumstances.

Broadly speaking, schools can tackle bullying in two different ways, which in effect reflect opposite sides of the same coin: firstly by directly focusing on the reduction of anti-social behaviour, and secondly by directly focusing on increasing pro-social behaviour. The former involves emphasising to pupils the harm caused by anti-social behaviour. The latter involves encouraging pupils to build up positive social relationships, recognising the rights of other pupils, and emphasising the importance of trust and cooperation. The interesting aspect of the pro-social approach is that it need not in effect mention bullying directly. Indeed, a number of activities covered by the PSHE curriculum and in the programme of study for citizenship can play a very important part in promoting pro-social behaviour that can effectively reduce bullying, and in particular in undermining the admiration and respect for bullying behaviour that can sometimes develop amongst certain groups of pupils.

A number of anti-bullying programmes include advice on ways in which bullying can be addressed as part of the PSHE curriculum. For example, the DFE pack lists a number of key questions that can be explored:

- What is bullying?
- What causes people to bully each other?
- How does it feel to be bullied and to bully?
- What are the effects of bullying behaviour on bullied pupils, on pupils who bully others, and on bystanders?
- What would our school be like if bullying behaviour was acceptable?
- Why should we try not to bully each other?
- What can we do to stop bullying?
- What moral dilemmas do we face when we are confronted with bullying behaviour?

Racial and sexual bullying

Some studies have focused specifically on bullying involving racial or sexual harassment. For example, Rivers (1995) used a questionnaire to explore the victimisation of 44 gay teenagers who were bullied at school. The most frequent form of bullying they reported was being ridiculed and called names. Interestingly, five respondents said that the bullying behaviour had taken place in front of teachers who had not attempted to intervene. Ofsted (2002) has commented that good school policies on bullying clearly state the school's stance and the action taken when racist or homophobic incidents occur.

Douglas and Warwick (2001) note that pupils who become targeted for homophobic bullying may, as a result, truant and have a lowered academic attainment. Their advice is that combating homophobic bullying needs to be included in the overall whole-school approach to tackling bullying. This requires the school to acknowledge that some bullying may be homophobic, and to consider action that can specifically target this form of bullying. For example, within the PSHE curriculum in secondary schools, pupils could consider topics such as:

- the positive and negative views held of men and women who are heterosexual, lesbian, gay and bisexual
- the pressures that face lesbians, gay men and bisexual people
- the effects of homophobia on pupils in school.

An example that might be useful here includes strategies for giving pupils a voice, such as:

- having a school council or similar forum for pupils to raise issues and suggest action
- providing pupils with anonymous ways of expressing their views – such as 'concern boxes' (secure mail boxes located around the school where pupils can bring issues to the attention of teachers through anonymous notes)

- enabling pupils to have access to staff other than teachers who can provide a confidential service (such as a school nurse, counsellor, learning mentor, personal adviser or youth worker)
- using participatory classroom activities that enable pupils to make their views known.

A distinction needs to be made between pupils using homophobic terms as terms of general abuse and the bullying of pupils because their appearance, manner or behaviour is suggestive of a gay or lesbian sexual orientation. Whilst the former can be more easily addressed by a general school policy to combat bullying, the latter will require some careful consideration of how best to protect and support pupils who are targeted because of their possible sexual orientation. A number of schools specifically address name calling as an issue, and will include in this context the unacceptability within the school community of any name calling and teasing based on references to race, sex and sexuality.

Homophobic bullying is a particularly sensitive area for schools to deal with. The development of a pupil's sexual identity is a gradual process that needs to be handled with great care. Issues to do with homosexuality will not have been considered to any great extent by many pupils towards the end of Year 11, and providing a forum for such issues to be discussed, and in particular providing opportunities for disclosure, can have unfortunate consequences, both in terms of raising the issue of homophobic bullying in a way that ends up encouraging it further, and in terms of leading pupils to disclose worries and concerns about their own sexuality that can make them a target of such bullying. Homophobic bullying certainly needs to be dealt with as part of the school's anti-bullying activities, but it is not at all clear whether addressing more general issues of homophobia within the PSHE curriculum would be beneficial.

Inter-agency cooperation

It is also interesting to note that a number of initiatives to combat bullying now involve coordinated action between different agencies, including schools, charities and mental heath services, which together have done much to raise public awareness of bullying as an issue, and to provide information for pupils and parents about various sources and forms of advice and help (face-to-face, telephone helplines and websites).

Whole-school anti-bullying policy

This involves providing staff with an agreed framework for intervention and prevention. All staff, pupils and parents need to be involved in this, and copies should be easily accessible in the staffroom and school library.

A positive school ethos

Programmes to create a positive school climate in which pupils recognise how their actions might upset others, whether this is intentional or not, and which establishes a need for pupils to act positively towards each other, can have a very effective impact on bullying. The danger of a school policy that simply targets bullies is that it relies overmuch on being able to identify bullies, and the identification process itself can raise the bully's status in the eyes of their peers.

Don't jump to conclusions

Listen carefully to what those involved in an incident have to say and try to get corroboration from others.

Tackling bullying through the curriculum

Teaching about bullying involves raising awareness about bullying behaviour and the school's anti-bullying policy, challenging attitudes about bullying, and building an anti-bullying ethos in the school. This can make use of videos, role-play, poetry, creative writing, and fiction.

Quality circles

Quality circles involve pupils working in groups to identify problems and come up with solutions (Mosley and Tew, 1999). There are five key steps involved in the process, which form a cycle:

- Identify the problem.
- Analyse the problem.
- Develop a solution.
- Present the solution.
- Review the solution.

Monitoring

Monitoring incidents of bullying enables patterns to be identified, particularly in relation to those involved, and when and where incidents occur. Monitoring needs to include reports by both teaching and non-teaching staff.

Mediation

Mediation involves helping the bully and victim to jointly resolve the problem of bullying that has arisen. Three well-known approaches are *shared concern, no blame* and *peer counselling* (see below).

Shared-concern approach

This approach, devised by Pikas (1989), encourages bullies to see the bullying as a problem that needs solving. Pikas focuses on 'mobbing', which he refers to as group violence. In the first stage the teacher has a 'non-confrontational chat' with the group of bullies, in which each bully is seen individually for about 10–20 minutes. The teacher follows a structured script which leads to each bully agreeing that the victim is unhappy and agreeing to help improve the situation, either by leaving the victim alone or being friendly towards them. In the next stage, the teacher has a supportive chat with the victim. In the case of 'provocative victims' the teacher helps them to understand how their behaviour contributed to the problem and advises them on how to change it. The third stage, after about a week, is to see each bully again either individually or as a group. The group talk may or may not involve the victim at this stage. In the fourth stage, all the pupils involved will meet together and publicly agree to behave reasonably in future. The shared-concern approach requires the teacher to be well trained in its use and to closely follow a script developed by Pikas.

No-blame approach

This approach is similar, but is less demanding than the shared-concern approach in terms of the training required and the procedure that needs to be followed. Robinson and Maines (1998) describe seven steps in the no-blame approach:

- Talk with the victim.
- Convene a meeting with the people involved.
- Explain the problem.
- Share responsibility.
- Ask the group members for their ideas.
- Leave it up to them.
- Meet them again.

Peer counselling

Peer-counselling schemes encourage victims to tell a peer counsellor if they are being bullied. Pupils who are willing to act as a peer counsellor are trained in active listening skills and given guidance on the ground rules

31

for their role. They then offer themselves 'on duty' during lunchtimes for one-to-one chats, either in a drop-in base room or by informal contact.

School counsellors

The number of schools that have a trained school counsellor is pitifully small, but studies have indicated that school counsellors can reduce bullying in schools (Ma *et al.*, 2001). In particular, school counsellors can help bullies to cope with their frustrations better and to develop conflict-resolution skills. They can also help victims to develop strategies that lessen the chance of peer rejection, and to improve their ability to interpret and deal effectively with hostile behaviour towards them.

Involving bystanders

Much bullying is witnessed by pupils who are not involved. These pupils can be encouraged to take a stand against bullying by telling the bully to stop what they are doing or showing their disapproval in some way, reporting the incident to a teacher, and befriending and involving the victim in some activity with their group. Bystanders can be shown how being passive can encourage bullying and how intervening can discourage bullying (Salmivalli, 1999).

Assertiveness training for victims

Some attempts have been made to encourage victims to develop assertiveness by role-play exercises in which they refuse to act compliant and submissive when teased or intimidated. This can empower victims to respond to a bullying situation without violence, and in a way that de-escalates the situation. A victim might be encouraged to use assertive phrases such as 'I don't like what you are doing and I want you to stop'. Lines (2001) has argued that developing a victim's ability to respond to teasing or name calling by using a put-down or making a humorous remark can be effective.

Targeting pupils at risk of becoming victims

Some pupils are particularly at risk of becoming victims of bullying. For example, pupils who have a speech defect are very likely to be teased about this. Teachers should thus be particularly vigilant in checking whether such pupils are being victimised and should explore with them what coping strategies they can use to prevent bullying occurring. Indeed, in the case of some pupils with special educational needs, advice on using resilient coping strategies to deal with bullying can make a huge difference in preventing them from becoming a victim.

Preventing bullying in the playground

Lunchtime supervisors are crucial here and should receive guidance and training on their role in combating bullying. Lunchtime supervisors need to

avoid labelling and be able to intervene in conflict situations. A well-planned playground also helps by making play attractive, thereby keeping pupils active rather than bored, since bullying can often arise when pupils are looking for some relief from boredom. In addition, encouraging play can help improve relationships.

References

Austin, S. and Joseph, S. (1996) 'Assessment of bully/victim problems in 8 to 11 year-olds.' *British Journal of Educational Psychology*, 66(4), 447–56.

Borg, M. G. (1998) 'The emotional reactions of school bullies and their victims.' *Educational Psychology*, 18(4), 433–44.

Boulton, M. J. (1997) 'Teachers' views on bullying: definitions, attitudes and ability to cope.' *British Journal of Educational Psychology*, 67(2), 223–33.

Boulton, M. J. and Underwood, K. (1992) 'Bully/victim problems among middle school children.' *British Journal of Educational Psychology*, 62(1), 73–87.

Branwhite, T. (1994) 'Bullying and student distress: beneath the tip of the iceberg.' *Educational Psychology*, 14(1), 59–71.

Crozier, W. R and Skliopidou, E. (2002) 'Adult recollections of name-calling at school.' *Educational Psychology*, 22(1), 113–24.

Cullingford, C. and Brown, G. (1995) 'Children's perceptions of victims and bullies.' *Education 3 to 13*, 23(2), 11–16.

DFE (1994) *Bullying: Don't Suffer in Silence.* London: HMSO.

DfES (2002) *Bullying.* DfES website: www.dfes.gov.uk/a-z/home.html.

Douglas, N. and Warwick, I. (2001) *Safe for All: A Best Practice Guide to Prevent Homophobic Bullying in Secondary Schools.* London: Citizenship 21 Project.

Guerin, S. and Hennessy, E. (2002) *Aggression and Bullying.* Oxford: BPS Blackwell.

Juvonen, J., Nishina, A. and Graham, S. (2000) 'Peer harassment, psychological adjustment, and school functioning in early adolescence.' *Journal of Educational Psychology*, 92(2), 349–59.

Lines, D. (2001) 'An approach with name-calling and verbal taunting.' *Pastoral Care in Education*, 18(1), 3–9.

Ma, X., Stewin, L. L. and Mah, D. (2001) 'Bullying in school: nature, effects and remedies.' *Research Papers in Education*, 16(3), 247–70.

Mosley, J. and Tew, M. (1999) *Quality Circle Time in the Secondary School.* London: David Fulton.

Ofsted (2002) *The Annual Report of Her Majesty's Chief Inspector of Schools 1999–2000: Standards and Quality in Education.* London: The Stationery Office.

Olweus, D. (1993) *Bullying at School: What We Know and What We Can Do.* Oxford: Blackwell.

Olweus, D. (1996) 'Bully/victim problems in school.' *Prospects*, 26(2), 331–59.

Pateraki, L. and Houndoumadi, A. (2001) 'Bullying among primary school children in Athens, Greece.' *Educational Psychology*, 21(2), 167–75.

Pikas, A. (1989) 'The common concern method for the treatment of mobbing.' In E. Roland and E. Munthe (eds) *Bullying: An International Perspective* (pp. 91–104). London: David Fulton.

Rigby, K. (2001) *Stop the Bullying: A Handbook for Schools.* London: David Fulton.

Rivers, I. (1995) 'The victimization of gay teenagers in schools: homophobia in education.' *Pastoral Care in Education*, 13(1), 35–41.

Robinson, G. and Maines, B. (1998) *Crying for Help: The No Blame Approach to Bullying.* Bristol: Lucky Duck Publishing.

Roland, E. (2002) 'Bullying, depressive symptoms and suicidal thoughts.' *Educational Research*, 44(1), 55–67.

Salmivalli, C. (1999) 'Participant role approach to school bullying: implications for interventions.' *Journal of Adolescence*, 22(4), 453–9.

Salmon, G., James, A., Cassidy, E. L. and Javaloyes, M. A. (2000) 'Bullying: a review. Presentations to an adolescent psychiatric service and within a school for emotionally and behaviourally disturbed children.' *Clinical Child Psychology and Psychiatry*, 5(4), 563–79.

SCRE (1992) *Action Against Bullying: A Support Pack for Schools.* Edinburgh: Scottish Council for Research in Education.

SCRE (1993) *Supporting Schools Against Bullying: The Second SCRE Anti-Bullying Pack.* Edinburgh: Scottish Council for Research in Education.

Sewell, K. (1999) 'Factors affecting one secondary school's efforts to combat bully/ victim problems.' DPhil thesis, University of York.

Sharp, S. and Thompson, D. (2001) *Bullying: Effective Strategies for Long-term Change.* London: RoutledgeFalmer.

Smith, P. K. and Levan, S. (1995) 'Perceptions and experiences of bullying in younger pupils.' *British Journal of Educational Psychology*, 65(4), 489–500.

Smith, P. K. and Sharp, S. (eds) (1994) *School Bullying: Insights and Perspectives.* London: Routledge.

Smith, P. K., Madsen, K. C. and Moody, J. C. (1999a) 'What causes the age decline in reports of being bullied at school? Towards a developmental analysis of risks of being bullied.' *Educational Research*, 41(3), 267–85.

Smith, P. K., Morita, Y., Catalano, R., Junger-Tas, J., Olweus, D. and Slee, P. (eds) (1999b) *The Nature of School Bullying: A Cross-National Perspective.* London: Routledge.

Stevens, V., De Bourdeaudhuij, I. and Van Oost, P. (2000) 'Bullying in Flemish schools: an evaluation of anti-bullying intervention in primary and secondary schools.' *British Journal of Educational Psychology*, 70(2), 195–210.

Stuart, M. and McCullagh, T. (1996) 'Bullying: the Northern Ireland context.' *Pastoral Care in Education*, 14(4), 25–9.

Weaver, A. (2000) 'Can post-traumatic stress disorder be diagnosed in adolescence without a catastrophic stressor? A case report.' *Clinical Child Psychology and Psychiatry*, 5(1), 77–83.

Whitney, I. and Smith, P. K. (1993) 'Bullying in junior/middle and secondary schools.' *Educational Research*, 35(1), 3–25.

4 Truancy

Truancy is one of the most pressing challenges facing education. It has a cost both for the individual who truants and for society as a whole, by contributing to low educational attainment, decreased life chances and criminal activity. The level of truancy also acts as an indicator of the health of the education system. If pupils feel that the education provided at school has little meaning or relevance for them and as a result do not attend school, then we need to think of initiatives and intervention programmes that can combat this. An inclusive society needs to do whatever it can to prevent pupils becoming marginalised by poor attainment and disaffection. It is small wonder then that as part of efforts to improve educational attainment in schools and reduce social exclusion in adulthood, there are a host of strategies in place to reduce truancy.

What do we mean by 'truancy' and 'school refusal' and how common are they?

Authorised absence is absence with permission from a teacher or other authorised representative of the school. This includes instances of absences for which a satisfactory explanation has been provided (e.g. illness). Unauthorised absence is absence without permission from a teacher or other authorised representative of the school. This includes all unexplained or unjustified absences. The DfES (1999) provides guidelines for schools concerning the categories of authorised and unauthorised absence.

The term 'truancy' refers to a pupil being absent from school without a legitimate reason (unauthorised absence). This may sound like a simple term to define, but researchers attempting to collect data on truancy often find it very difficult to draw up a set of categories of behaviour where it is unequivocally clear whether a particular case counts as truancy or not. Here are the five main categories used:

Pure truancy

Here the pupil simply does not turn up at school and the parents think the pupil has gone to school.

Parentally condoned truancy

Here the pupil does not turn up at school but the parents are aware of this and also aware that there is no legitimate reason for the absence. For example, the pupil might have spent the day helping a parent with some task at the parent's place of work, or looking after someone who was at home ill. Some parents will allow a child to stay at home if it is the child's birthday. The essence of this category is that the parent is aware that the child is not at school and also aware that the reason for this is not legitimate. However, this category does beg the question of what counts as legitimate. Reid (2002) notes that this group includes a mix of different types of parents, some of whom can be regarded as anti-education, others who are simply weak and condone whatever their children want to do, and others who are dependent on their children for help and support and need to have them at home.

Parentally duped truancy

Here the pupil manages to persuade their parents that they are sufficiently ill not to be able to attend school, when in fact they are quite well. The parent will then write a letter to excuse the pupil's absence on grounds of ill health. This category is often hard to distinguish from parentally condoned truancy, since some parents are much more willing than others to accept a simple declaration of not feeling well as sufficient and may in large measure be conniving with their child rather than being genuinely duped.

Post-registration truancy

This category (sometimes also referred to as 'internal truancy') includes pupils who go to school, gain an attendance mark in the school register, but then miss one or more lessons during the school day, sometimes remaining on the school premises, or leaving it for short periods of time.

School refusal

This category refers to pupils who are psychologically disturbed by the idea of going to school (Heyne and Rollings, 2002; Place *et al.*, 2000). This includes conditions stemming from problems at school, such as finding the work too difficult, or being bullied, and to psychiatric conditions such as school phobia or depression. Here the pupil is clearly so upset by the idea of going to school that there is little that the parent can do to persuade them to attend, and some degree of counselling intervention will be needed. Again, however, there is a thin line between those pupils who are genuinely disturbed and those who simply refuse to go to school because they do not want to and whose parents are unable to make them go.

Estimating the incidence of truancy

The problems involved in assessing and recording truancy make it very difficult to get an accurate picture of the frequency of truancy. One indicator is simply to look at the rates of school attendance. For example, on any one day, school attendance is typically around 94 per cent for primary schools and 91 per cent for secondary schools. Overall, attendance seems to be lowest in the last two years of compulsory schooling (Years 10 and 11). In both primary and secondary schools, girls are more likely to be absent than boys. However, the vast majority of non-attendance is due to genuine illnesses.

When we explore those absences that can be deemed to constitute truancy, it is estimated that the national rate for truancy based on the official statistics of percentage of half-days missed because of unauthorised absence is 0.5 per cent for primary schools and 1 per cent for secondary schools (DfES, 2002a). When a correction is made for truancy that occurs but is not officially recorded, this estimate rises to 1 per cent for primary schools and 3.5 per cent for secondary schools. About 80 per cent of the truants are male.

A study by Galloway (1976) looked at a group of pupils with poor attendance from 30 secondary schools and their feeder primary schools in Sheffield. Galloway identified 233 primary school pupils and 639 secondary school pupils who had missed at least 50 per cent of the possible attendance over a seven-week period in the first half of an autumn term, whom he labelled 'persistent absentees'. He reported that truancy, defined as absence without the knowledge or consent of the parent (i.e. *pure truancy*), accounted for 2 per cent of the persistent absentees in primary schools and 11 per cent in secondary schools. This study indicates that only a small minority of persistent absentees fall into the category of pure truancy, and the most frequent reason for persistent absence is genuine illness.

A number of writers, however, have indicated that the number of authorised absences recorded by schools may be unreliable for many reasons, not least because schools are under a lot of pressure to meet targets for attendance set for them. Reid (2002) has noted a number of ways in which schools fail to record unauthorised absences. For example, he noted that some schools offer pupils who returned to school after an absence a form on which they are asked to tick a box selecting the reason for their absence.

Some studies have estimated levels of truancy by looking at self-reported data. For example, Beinart *et al.* (2002) carried out a survey based on a questionnaire completed by 14,445 secondary school pupils aged 11 to 16 years in England, Scotland and Wales. They reported that truancy rose steeply with age. Some 7 per cent of girls and 11 per cent of boys in Year 7 (aged 11 to 12 years) said they had truanted in the previous year, compared with 41 per cent of girls and 38 per cent of boys in Year 11 (aged 15 to 16 years). Most who had taken unauthorised absence said it only involved occasional lessons, but 16 per cent of boys and 18 per cent of girls in Year 11 reported taking off whole days or longer. In addition, Beinart *et al.* reported that 42 per cent of the Year 11 pupils thought it was easy to truant from their school, which suggests that in a number of schools the policies and procedures in place to combat truancy are not perceived by many pupils as effective in making truancy difficult. Twenty-one per cent of the Year 11 pupils reported that they had truanted in the previous four weeks, and Beinhart *et al.* note that this figure almost certainly underestimates the true percentage, as the questionnaires were completed in school time and consequently some truants would not have been there to complete it.

The Social Exclusion Unit (1998) argued that truancy had reached a crisis point. It noted that official figures in 1997 indicated that about one million pupils (around 15 per cent of all pupils) had taken at least one half-day off without authority. Moreover, it observed that there was a marked difference between these official figures and surveys of young people which indicate a far higher level of truancy. It noted that surveys of pupils indicate that about 30 per cent of pupils in Years 10 and 11 admitted truanting at least once in the previous half-term, and that the vast majority of truants had engaged in post-registration truancy. It also noted some 'hot spots'. For example, attendance fell below 50 per cent for a fifth of primary school age traveller children and a third of secondary school age, and that many traveller children were not even registered at school.

Truancy and educational attainment

The DfES (2001a) Youth Cohort Study looked at the educational qualifications achieved by a sample of 16-year-olds in England and Wales and what they were doing some eight months after completing compulsory education. The data were based on questionnaires completed by 13,698 pupils. The extent of truancy admitted by this sample is shown in Table 4.1. As can be seen, about 4 per cent of the sample were categorised as persistent truants in Year 11, and of these only 10 per cent gained five or more GCSEs at grades A* to C, and 21 per cent of these gained no GCSEs at all. This compares with 58 per cent and 3 per cent respectively for those who had never truanted in Year 11.

Table 4.1 Reported truancy in Year 11 and GCSE attainment

Truancy in Year 11	% of the sample	% who gained 5 or more GCSE grades A*–C	% who gained no GCSEs
Persistent truants	4	10	21
For weeks at a time	2		
For several days or lessons	2		
Occasional truants	31	38	5
For particular days or lessons	6		
For the odd day or lesson	25		
Never	65	58	3

Source: DfES (2001a)

These figures indicate that persistent truants were seven times more likely to achieve no GCSEs at all compared with non-truants. Nevertheless, it is also important to note that as many as 10 per cent of the persistent truants did do well, which suggests that a sizeable proportion of persistent truants may be able, and we should not stereotype this group as solely comprising pupils who are unable to achieve a good level of academic success. However, it is worth bearing in mind that the study does require a fairly long questionnaire to be completed, and the response rate of those surveyed was 55 per cent, so it is likely that the persistent truants who completed the questionnaire may not be fully representative of the total population of persistent truants, and are likely to be more able than those persistent truants who did not respond.

Variation in truancy between schools

Looking at data on truancy as a whole fails to highlight the enormous variation between schools in levels of attendance and truancy. Ofsted (2002) rated attendance as 'unsatisfactory or poor' at 17 per cent of primary schools and at 22 per cent of secondary schools. Ofsted was particularly critical of families who take long holidays during term time. Its inspection reports on individual schools published on the Ofsted website include reports on attendance at some schools where the level of internal truancy was so great that teachers often had no idea which pupils they were to expect at their lessons.

Persistent truancy

It will be evident from the various research studies and official statistics that it is difficult to estimate how big a problem truanting is. Any estimate will need to take some account of how serious each case is. If we included as truanting every pupil who had missed at least one lesson in a school year in any of the five categories listed above, the proportion of pupils classified as truanting would suggest this was now a national epidemic. For example, in Year 11, between a third and a half of all pupils would be identified as truants. If, at the other extreme, we focused just on serious cases of pure truanting, the proportion of pupils classified in this way would appear almost negligible in primary schools, and in secondary schools would reach about 10 per cent by Years 10 and 11.

Our estimate (shown in Table 4.2) is based on how many pupils are missing lessons on a regular enough basis (say equivalent to more than 50 hours in a given school term) to be giving rise to serious concern. This is not, of course, to say that any unjustified missing of a single lesson is not to be treated seriously, but including all cases of minor truanting distorts attempts to estimate the scale of the problem.

What are the main causes of truancy and school refusal?

A number of studies have explored the reasons given by truants for not attending school (Malcolm *et al.*, 1995; Reid, 1999). The most frequent reasons reported were:

- The lessons were boring.
- The work was too difficult.

Table 4.2 An estimate of 'serious truanting' in terms of the number of pupils per 1000 who are unjustifiably absent from school for more than 50 hours in a single term

	Primary schools Years 1–6	Secondary schools Years 7–9	Secondary schools Years 10–11
Pure truancy	1	5	40
Parentally condoned truancy	1	3	24
Parentally duped truancy	1	1	8
Post-registration truancy	0.5	2.5	20
School refusal	1	1	8

- They had problems with particular teachers.
- The school atmosphere was too strict.
- They felt rejected by the school.
- The school did not offer them enough personal attention.
- They were being bullied.
- They wanted to spend time with friends or on their own.
- The school curriculum was not relevant.

For example, Smith (1996) conducted a questionnaire survey of 6411 secondary school pupils in Hertfordshire regarding school attendance. He reported that truanting gradually increased from Year 7, where 3 per cent of pupils said they truanted frequently (i.e. more than three times a half-term), to Year 11, where 18 per cent of pupils truanted frequently. The pupils gave four main reasons for truanting:

- lesson difficulty
- bullying
- not liking school
- peer pressure.

The Social Exclusion Unit (1998) noted that truancy was affected by problems at school. It noted four examples of this:

- In some schools, poor attendance was centred amongst weak readers.
- Non-attendance can be the result of anxiety about GCSE coursework deadlines.
- About a third of girls and a quarter of boys are afraid to go to school at some time because of bullying.
- Some pupils truant because they dislike particular lessons or teachers or see school or the National Curriculum as irrelevant.

In addition, it argued that poor parental supervision and a lack of commitment to education are crucial factors behind truancy. It noted that about 40 per cent of truants believed their parents knew they were truanting. It also noted that for boys, living in a single-parent family is a particular risk factor.

A study by Graham and Bowling (1995) was based on questionnaires completed by 2529 subjects aged 14 to 25 years. Thirty-seven per cent of the males and 28 per cent of the females said they had skipped school for at least one day without permission. The study looked at the correlates of truancy, and found these to be broadly similar for both sexes:

- poor parental supervision
- a lack of attachment to family and siblings
- having friends in trouble with the police.

Graham and Bowling found that, overall, family influence was the most important factor associated with truancy. Truants more often have parents who sometimes do not know where their children are or whom they are with, and they more often have poor relationships with their parents. They note that although a number of measures have been introduced to reduce truancy, more attention needs to be given to the responsibility of parents, and that when evidence of persistent absenteeism begins to accumulate, parents need to be contacted and involved sooner rather than later, particularly in view of the link between truancy and poor parental supervision. Graham and Bowling also note that pupils who truant in primary school often bring this reputation with them when they transfer to secondary school, and they argue that the 'fresh start' offered when pupils begin secondary school needs to be capitalised on so that this reputation is not re-established in their new school.

Kinder *et al.* (1995) used interviews to explore the views of senior managers, heads of year and form tutors in 30 schools and special units and of some LEA and education welfare personnel concerning the causes of disaffection, truancy and disruption. They grouped the reported causes of truancy into three main areas:

- *Individual pathologies or personality traits.* These included low self-esteem, poor social skills, low confidence, low academic ability, special needs, poor concentration and poor self-management skills.

- *Family circumstances or values and/or social factors within the non-attenders' communities.* These included parents who do not value education and do not appear to be concerned about poor attendance; significant domestic problems, inadequate or inconsistent parenting; living in a community with high unemployment and economic deprivation.

- *School factors, often located in either the curriculum or the ethos and relationships encountered there by pupils.* These included problems with particular teachers; poor relationships with peers; not seeing what the school offers as relevant; academic failure; the lack of flexibility in the National Curriculum and assessment procedures to better meet these pupils' needs and interests; lack of school time for pastoral provision.

Pupils' feeling about truanting

Another important aspect of truancy is the range of pupils' emotional responses to missing school. For example, when pupils are asked how they feel when committing truancy in terms of five categories of response, the largest proportion, about half, report having 'no feelings'. The remainder, however, are equally divided between those feeling excited, proud, guilty and ashamed. These differences often reflect the circumstances which have led to the truancy. For example, a pupil who missed school because they did not have the money to pay for the ingredients in a food technology class or because they did not have a clean PE kit is likely to feel ashamed. However, the fact that the category chosen by the largest number is 'no feelings' suggests a certain bareness of habit, in which truants neither take any real pleasure in truanting nor feel any remorse in doing so. For them, truanting is just a habit.

Indeed, a number of writers have pointed out that the first time someone truants from school there is often a clear reason. This may be that they are being bullied at school, have not done their homework, or need to look after a sick relative, or perhaps it is an act of bravado with a friend. What is crucial is what happens afterwards. If the school and/or the parents do not discover the true reasons for the absence, or do not seem particularly bothered, then further truanting can occur for no particular reason, and before long truanting can become just a habit. The more the pupil truants, the harder it becomes for the truant to cope with the work at school or to feel part of a network of friends at school, and this then creates a vicious circle in which truanting fuels further disaffection.

Truancy and preferred learning styles

Rayner and Riding (1996) conducted a study looking at the preferred learning styles of 17 school refusers aged from 15 to 17 years who were attending a special unit for pupils who refused to attend school. All these pupils had a statement of special educational needs and had an established history of truancy. The holistic–analytic learning style dimension distinguishes those who prefer to process information as a whole from those who prefer to process information in parts. Rayner and Riding found that 47 per cent of the school refusers were holistic, compared with only 6 per cent who were analytic, with the remainder categorised as intermediate. One cause of truancy might be that truants are frustrated by certain types of learning activities and approaches. Rayner and Riding argue therefore that one part of combating truancy may involve trying to tailor truants' learning experiences to their preferred learning style, and in particular being alert to the possibility that most truants find it difficult to learn in a style that focuses too much on details.

School refusers

The distinction between truants and school refusers, although sometimes blurred, is an important one. School refusal is a broad category, which includes both those who have developed a strong fear of going to school for understandable reasons, such as persistent bullying and wanting to avoid repeated failure, and those for whom this fear appears largely irrational or unexplainable. This latter group are sometimes diagnosed as suffering from *separation anxiety*, characterised by excessive worries about what will happen if they are not with their parents, or as suffering from *school phobia*, characterised by an irrational fear of the school or some aspect of features located within the school. What all school refusers have in common, however, is an intense emotional and behavioural reaction against the idea of going to school. The symptoms may include vomiting, complaining of aches and pains, extreme anxiety, and shouting and screaming their refusal if the parents try to force or coerce them to go. Heyne and Rollings (2002) have highlighted four ways in which school refusers typically differ from pure truants:

- They do not attempt to conceal their absence from parents.
- Their non-attendance lasts for prolonged periods (weeks or months) rather than being intermittent.
- They are academically sound and have vocational goals which require schooling.
- They are generally well behaved.

A study by Cooper and Mellors (1991) looked at the views of 26 teachers working in special teaching units in the South East of England concerning truants and school refusers. Almost all the school refusers were seen as being emotionally disturbed, particularly in terms of being anxious, timid, shy and emotionally withdrawn, whereas hardly any of the truants were viewed in this way. Conversely, the most frequent characteristic of truants was seen to be anti-social behaviour. Such differences have important implications for the type of support such pupils will need if they are to be successfully reintegrated into school.

What can schools do to help truants and school refusers and to reduce truancy and school refusal?

A great deal has been written about approaches that schools can take to minimise truancy (Collins, 1998; Hallam, 1996, 1997; Reid, 1999). These focus on better monitoring and support for pupils at risk of truanting, and adapting the curriculum to better suit their needs. Liaison with outside agencies and the threat of legal proceedings can also play a helpful part here. Ofsted (2002) reported that procedures for monitoring attendance were effective in a majority of secondary schools, and that action to improve attendance was more effective when it was linked with promoting good behaviour and attainment, where weak excuses for absence were not accepted, and where the importance of not missing lessons was stressed to parents and pupils.

Collins (1998) analysed information gathered from 20 secondary schools, from which four schools were then studied in depth. He categorised this information into six themes:

- communication with parents on attendance matters
- methods used to motivate pupils to attend
- recognising, categorising and recording absences

- communications with parents on unauthorised absences
- measures used by the schools to deal with unauthorised absences
- engaging the help of outside agencies.

Collins reported that none of the 20 schools had an agreed and published policy on attendance and that key information for parents regarding attendance was often missing or unclear. The teachers felt that the National Curriculum targets sometimes promoted truancy, because low-ability, troublesome and impulsive pupils responded to evidence of their failure to achieve the goals set by going absent. The schools also found it difficult to identify unauthorised absences because of the complex mix of information, parental notes and records of phone calls involved. To some extent there was also a disincentive for schools to identify unauthorised absences as this is a negative school performance indicator, so schools have a vested interest in underestimating it. Communications with parents to investigate an absence were often time consuming and rushed, and some parents were judged as being uncooperative. What parents said was often accepted at face value, and in some cases where there appeared to be a family breakdown, illness or other crisis occurring, schools colluded with parents in condoning unauthorised absences. In some cases, parents were not able to control their children, and teachers were torn between compensating for this by on the one hand being sympathetic and supportive to the pupil and offering rewards for improving attendance, and on the other hard being firm, critical and punishing of absence in order to keep the pressure on pupils to attend. The expectations that schools had in referring a case to the education welfare service (EWS) were often unclear. In some cases schools simply wanted further information on the reason for the absence whilst in other cases it was being assumed that the EWS would be taking action to improve attendance.

Intervention projects

A number of practical projects have been undertaken in schools to combat truancy. One secondary school issued the following warning to pupils who are tempted to take a day off school:

When I am off school for just one day it may mean:

- I'll fall behind with my school work
- I'll get poor GCSE grades
- I'll find it harder to make and keep friends
- I might get bullied
- I'll miss out on school events
- I won't be a school prefect
- I might get in trouble with the police
- I might not get the job I want or be able to go to college
- I won't fulfil my potential.

Other projects have involved the following:

- rewards or incentives for pupils who achieve 100 per cent attendance over a specified period, such as certificates, stationery items, cinema, football and swimming vouchers
- engaging local football clubs in backing good attendance schemes and awarding the certificates and prizes
- a competitive system of comparing attendance rates of the tutor groups at the end of each week
- the issue of a pass to pupils who are out of school with permission to operate in conjunction with a truancy watch scheme
- activities with parents which highlight their role in promoting attendance.

Taken as a whole what these schemes do is to create a climate in the school in which attendance is expected and rewarded, and counters the development of a subculture in which truanting is able to thrive.

The Social Exclusion Unit (1998) noted that the most effective anti-truancy measure is to act quickly and consistently, and always to contact parents immediately pupils are absent. This shows that the school does not tolerate truancy and means that parents cannot ignore it either. The Unit estimates that measures of this kind can quickly raise attendance by 5 to 10 per cent. It also notes five other ingredients of effective anti-truancy approaches:

- making a truancy crackdown an issue for the whole school – all pupils, all teachers, parents, ancillary staff and the local community, which can also be extended to 'truancy watch' schemes involving the police, local businesses and others
- unambiguous discipline policies, applied consistently to stamp out bullying and negative peer pressures
- computerised registration so schools can identify patterns and possible causes, for example particular groups of children who are truanting or particular lessons that are being missed
- dealing early with pupils' literacy and numeracy problems so they catch up academically, and offering an alternative curriculum for those unlikely to achieve at GCSE
- extra-curricular activities – such as after-school clubs, study support, vocational learning, work experience and education-business community links – to motivate pupils at risk of becoming disaffected.

Whole-school policies to improve attendance

A number of schools have developed a whole-school policy to combat truancy, often designating a senior member of staff responsible for attendance. The DfES (2001b) cites four main benefits of such a policy:

- Responsibility for promoting school attendance is shared by everyone in the school, rather than being left to particular individuals or groups.

- Developing an attendance policy touches all aspects of a school's life, and relates directly to the school's values, ethos and curriculum.
- Opportunities arise for cost-effective networking and joint training involving groups of schools or different professional groups.
- Rigorous collection and analysis of data about attendance enables schools to check their progress against measurable outcomes.

Truancy and exclusion

It is interesting to note that truancy can sometimes lead to a permanent exclusion, despite the fact that DFE (1994) guidance on exclusions explicitly regards exclusion as an inappropriate response. Indeed, the DFE points out that exclusion in these circumstances could hinder effective action to tackle truancy. The DFE suggests that where truancy is a cause for concern, the school should work closely with the LEA education welfare officers to resolve the problem, and if the difficulties continue, the LEA could apply for an education supervision order or, where necessary, initiate legal proceedings against the parents.

Truancy and delinquency

It is the link between truancy and juvenile delinquency that frequently leads to heightened discussion in the media for urgent action to be taken by the government to crack down on truancy. A great deal of juvenile delinquency takes place during the school day whilst pupils are truanting from school. An estimated 50,000 pupils are absent from school without leave each day in England, and 40 per cent of street crime, 25 per cent of burglaries, 20 per cent of criminal damage and a third of all car thefts are carried out by 10–16-year-old pupils in school hours. Consequently, effective approaches to reduce truancy would at a stroke have a major impact on reducing crime. A number of initiatives have therefore been undertaken which address combating truancy as part of a crime-reduction programme. For example, in regions where crime is highest, a number of schools are involved in projects in which uniformed police will visit primary and secondary schools on a regular basis, patrol the playgrounds, talk to pupils, help improve school security and share information with teachers. In some cases, uniformed police officers will also talk to pupils as part of the PSHE and citizenship curriculum.

School–community protocols

The DfES (2002b) has produced a protocol for schools intended to provide a framework for the development of local protocols to establish effective programmes of joint working between schools, local police and partnership agencies. The purpose of the protocol is:

- to help promote dialogue and further develop effective partnerships between schools, police and other agencies that are based on cooperation and shared understandings

- to set expectations for local partnerships, while allowing police services and schools to address service-delivery arrangements and local circumstances
- to define the respective roles and responsibilities for the police, schools and partnership agencies.

The aim of the protocol should be to enhance the learning environment by providing a safe and secure school community and reducing street crime and anti-social behaviour. It should result in:

- young people feeling safe and valued
- young people engaged in education, actively learning and achieving at higher levels
- the lowest possible levels of bullying, intimidation and crime experienced by groups of young people.

The protocol should not be an end in itself, but a reflection of genuine understanding that enables police to be involved in schools on the basis of regular, visible and well-supported contacts that promote positive outcomes for school staff and pupils as well as the police and wider community.

Prosecuting parents

Some initiatives have targeted the parents of persistent truants. Reid (2002) notes that parents taken to court face fines of up to £2500 and can go to prison for up to three months, and that the government is exploring whether various additional measures can be more effective in pressuring such parents to ensure their children do not truant. In addition, some projects in areas of high crime include classes for parents of challenging pupils to help them develop the skills to help improve their children's behaviour and reduce truancy.

Combating disaffection

One of the major sources of truancy is that pupils feel forced to study subjects they have lost interest in. As a result they increasingly feel the school curriculum has little to offer them. A number of initiatives allow disaffected pupils to study vocationally oriented subjects, including outside school, in, for example, a further education college, in order to help prevent such disaffection occurring. In addition, the *Connexions Service* (DfES, 2002c), which began to be phased in during 2001, provides a multi-agency support service for all 13–19-year-old pupils, which brings together schools, colleges, career services, the youth service, the EWS, health agencies and youth offending teams in order to provide a coherent, holistic package of support to enable pupils to remain engaged in learning. The service will be a universal service but will give particular priority to those at greatest risk of not making a successful transition into learning and work in adult life. As well as ensuring all pupils receive personal advice and guidance, the service will provide personal advisers, some of whom will be based in schools and will target disaffected pupils. In particular, personal advisers will work with truants to encourage them to improve their attendance.

One of the reasons truants often give for truanting is that they dislike the school ethos. Schools are still places were pupils are largely regimented, in being told what to do and when, for most of the school day. Many pupils during adolescence increasingly find such regimentation oppressive. In addition, teacher–pupil relationships are still very much based on teachers being in authority. There is little doubt that the typical school ethos has gradually become more humanistic over the years, and that teachers' relations with pupils are generally much less authoritarian than they were in the past. Nevertheless, it is still the case that schools are regimented institutions. At the same time, children have been maturing faster, and many pupils are increasingly expecting to be treated more like adults during the secondary school years. Indeed, one common complaint that pupils have against teachers is that they are often treated as children and not more like adults. Whilst it is inevitable that a complex institution such as a school can only function smoothly if pupils' behaviour is regimented to a large extent, teachers can do more to soften what they say and how they deal with pupils so that pupils' sense of an oppressive and regimented school ethos can be lessened. This means that in dealing with truants, teachers need to focus more on helping pupils to understand why they should contract into schooling rather than simply rely on strategies based on coercion. Part of this contracting may involve dealing with truants in a more sensitive manner and trying to establish a more egalitarian relationship. To some extent, the idea of mentors and personal advisors for disaffected pupils builds on this approach in trying to encourage truants to attend school regularly.

Dealing with school refusal

Heyne and Rollings (2002) note that tackling school refusal needs to address the underlying problems that may be maintaining the pupil's anxieties. The pupil needs to be reassured that their fears about what will follow if they go to school are unfounded. Their parents need to identify which aspects of staying at home may be acting as rewards that reinforce school refusal and remove them. Finally, reassuring support needs to be put in place in the school setting.

ACTION POINTS

Monitoring attendance

The school needs to have procedures in place to identify and act quickly whenever truancy is suspected. It needs to monitor its own unique pattern of absences to identify individuals who may be truants. This may be linked with the days on which certain lessons occur. Electronic registers can also help identify patterns that may indicate truancy.

A whole-school policy to combat truancy

The advantage of a whole-school policy is two-fold. It raises awareness of the importance of attendance, and it enables procedures to be followed consistently and with rigour.

First day contact

Making contact with parents of pupils who are absent from school without prior knowledge on the day that the absence occurs is generally regarded as the single most effective action a school can take to combat truancy. Electronic recording of registration can allow text messages to be sent to parents' mobile phones automatically, and some commercial agencies offer a first-day contact service to schools in which they contact the parents on behalf of the school and pass the parents' responses back to the school.

Registration checks at start of lessons

In order to combat post-registration (internal) truancy, some schools will frequently make a registration check at the start of lessons, so that pupils who have gone missing can be identified. Electronic recording of registration can allow each teacher to check instantly for internal truancy at the start of a lesson.

Promoting a positive physical school environment

The physical environment needs to be clean, comfortable and welcoming.

Promoting a positive social school environment

The social environment needs to be positive, with good relationships and rapport promoted both between pupils and between pupils and teachers; in particular, the environment needs to be relatively free of bullying.

Support for academic difficulties

The educational environment needs to reflect a supportive school ethos and to help pupils having problems with their academic work.

Support for emotional and behavioural difficulties

The school needs to have a pastoral support system in place that can be swiftly brought into action when pupils encounter problems arising either at school or at home which can lead them to become upset, depressed or disaffected. This may show itself in a deterioration in their work or behaviour, which if not picked up quickly may lead to truancy.

Access to a relevant curriculum

Pupils are more likely to attend school if at least some of the work appears to be clearly relevant to their needs and offers them opportunities for success. In the later years of schooling, work which has a strong vocational relevance can help to improve attendance. Some compact schemes involving local employers have been used to link good attendance with work experience and employment opportunities.

Remedial activities

These activities aim to raise basic levels of literacy and numeracy so that pupils with poor skills in these areas who are at risk of truancy are better able to cope with the academic demands made on them. These activities will also include emotional support and encouragement aimed at helping to raise their self-esteem and confidence.

Offering an alternative working environment

Some schools have a working area set aside for pupils who are finding it difficult to work with teachers in a normal classroom setting; this working area may be used in place of particular lessons where problems have arisen, and may be used on a short-term basis until the pupil is able to readjust to the normal classroom environment. Such working areas may also operate before and after the normal school day.

Breakfast and homework clubs

These are working areas which operate for about one hour before and after the normal school day to provide an opportunity for pupils to complete academic tasks, and thereby to mitigate the truancy that arises because pupils have fallen behind with their work.

Offering reasons to attend

Entry to GCSEs and other qualifications, attractive curriculum activities, work placements and compacts with employers can give pupils positive reasons to improve attendance.

Education welfare officers

External agents, such as education welfare officers, can play a crucial role in helping to monitor problems that can give rise to truancy, and act as a link between home and school to help ensure that attendance is maintained.

Making use of preferred learning activities

All pupils have certain activities that they enjoy and others that they find difficult or boring. Attention needs to be given to enabling truants to learn in accordance with their preferred learning style where possible, and to

making them aware that they need to be more patient and persistent when their non-preferred activities are used.

Rewards for good attendance

Offering rewards for pupils who are poor attenders in order to encourage attendance can be useful. Such rewards may be symbolic, such as a certificate or a letter to parents, or tangible, such as a monetary token or pass to some leisure activity.

Discouraging families from taking holidays in term time

For some parents there may be pressing reasons why a family holiday needs to be taken during term time. However, where this is done casually and for general convenience it sends a message to their children and others that attendance at school is not essential. General guidance to parents about school attendance can usefully explain why it is important for absences to be kept to a minimum.

Truancy patrols and hotlines

These involve a senior teacher in the school patrolling the school site at various times throughout the day to deal with pupils who are not in lessons when they should be and to take them somewhere where they can be supervised. The pupil is normally warned that if they are caught out of lessons again their parents will be contacted and the pupil may be referred for in-school support. In addition, those in the local community are encouraged to report and challenge pupils who might be out of school without authorisation, and some schemes involve targeting areas in the locality where truants are known to hang about.

Support for reintegration

Pupils attempting to readjust to school after a period of absence need particular support. In particular, such pupils will need help to catch up on missed work (Howe, 1995; Tansey, 1995). Gullone and King (1991) describe a behavioural strategy to help school refusers return to school, which involves helping parents to ignore their child's complaints of sickness or headaches and deal with their child's protests and temper tantrums, and ensures that teachers provide plenty of support and encouragement for their work in school. A period of time spent in a school-based inclusion unit can be particularly helpful for truants and school refusers who have been away from school for a long period of time (the use of inclusion units is considered in the next chapter).

Inter-agency cooperation

A number of writers have highlighted the importance of inter-agency work in helping to deal with truants. Irving and Parker-Jenkins (1995) have suggested that truancy centres could provide a useful focus for such inter-agency work. However, such centres must not become the dumping ground for pupils that schools do not want. For truancy centres to be effective in combating truancy, they need to be seen as providing pupils with a short-term respite during which their needs can be assessed and plans can be made to reintegrate them into schools.

Prosecution

Legal proceedings can take various forms, including a school attendance order, an education supervision order, and the prosecution of the parents. Waddington (1997) explored the views of 27 education welfare officers concerning the impact of threatened and actual prosecution of parents on the officers' relationships with their clients (the parents and truants). About half the officers reported that this was helpful, whilst half thought that it had little or no effect, and in some cases could be harmful. Galloway (1985) also reported that legal proceedings for truancy have very mixed results. Nevertheless, the threat of legal proceedings can usefully serve to highlight the seriousness with which truancy is regarded, and can help motivate both parents and the truants to cooperate with efforts to secure attendance.

References

Beinart, S., Anderson, B., Lee, S. and Utting, D. (2002) *Youth at Risk? A National Survey of Risk Factors, Protective Factors and Problem Behaviour among Young People in England, Scotland and Wales.* London: Communities that Care.

Collins, D. (1998) *Managing Truancy in Schools.* London: Cassell.

Cooper, M. and Mellors, M. (1991) 'Teachers' perceptions of school refusers and truants.' *Educational Review*, 42(3), 319–26.

DFE (1994) *Exclusions from School (Circular 10/94).* London: DFE.

DfES (1999) *Social Inclusion: Pupil Support (Circular 10/99).* London: DfES.

DfES (2001a) *Youth Cohort Study. The Activities and Experiences of 16 Year Olds: England and Wales 2000.* London: DfES.

DfES (2001b) *Attendance and Absence.* DfES website: www.dfes.gov.uk/a-z/atozindex.html.

DfES (2002a) Pupil absences in England in the 2000/01 school year. DfES website: www.dfes.gov.uk.

DfES (2002b) *Police–School Protocols.* DfES website: www.teachernet.gov.uk/streetcrime.

DfES (2002c) *Connexions service.* DfES website: www.dfes.gov.uk/a-z/atozindex.html.

Galloway, D. (1976) 'Size of school, socio-economic hardship, suspension rates and persistent unjustified absence from school.' *British Journal of Educational Psychology*, 46(1), 40–7.

Galloway, D. (1985) *School and Persistent Absentees.* Oxford: Pergamon.

Graham, J. and Bowling, B. (1995) *Young People and Crime (Home Office Research Study 145).* London: Home Office.

Gullone, E. and King, N. J. (1991) 'Acceptability of alternative treatments for school refusal: evaluations by students, caregivers and professionals.' *British Journal of Educational Psychology*, 61(3), 346–54.

Hallam, S. (1996) *Improving School Attendance.* Oxford: Heinemann.

Hallam, S. (1997) *Truancy: Can Schools Improve Attendance? Viewpoint No. 6.* London: University of London Institute of Education.

Heyne, D. and Rollings, S. (2002) *School Refusal.* Oxford: BPS Blackwell.

Howe, D. (1995) 'Willingly to school? How the well-organized and welcoming school can combat unnecessary absence.' *Pastoral Care in Education*, 13(4), 29–31.

Irving, B. A. and Parker-Jenkins, M. (1995) 'Tackling truancy: an examination of persistent non-attendance amongst disaffected school pupils and positive support strategies.' *Cambridge Journal of Education*, 25(2), 225–35.

Kinder, K., Harland, J., Wilkin, A. and Wakefield, A. (1995) *Three to Remember: Strategies for Disaffected Pupils.* Slough: NFER.

Malcolm, H., Thorpe, G. and Lowden, K. (1995) *Understanding Truancy: Links between Attendance, Truancy and Performance.* Edinburgh: SCRE.

Ofsted (2002) *The Annual Report of Her Majesty's Chief Inspector of Schools 1999–2000: Standards and Quality in Education.* London: The Stationery Office.

Place, M., Hulsmeier, J., Davis, S. and Taylor, E. (2000) 'School refusal: a changing problem which requires a change of approach?' *Clinical Child Psychology and Psychiatry*, 5(3), 345–55.

Rayner, S. and Riding, R. (1996) 'Cognitive style and school refusal.' *Educational Psychology*, 16(4), 445–51.

Reid, K. (1999) *Tackling Truancy in Schools.* London: Routledge.

Reid, K. (2002) *Truancy: Short and Long-term Solutions.* London: RoutledgeFalmer.

Smith, M. (1996) 'School attendance in Hertfordshire.' *Educational Research*, 38(2), 226–36.

Social Exclusion Unit (1998) *Truancy and School Exclusion.* London: The Stationery Office.

Tansey, K. (1995) 'This can't be my responsibility: it must be yours! An analysis of a reintegration programme for a school refuser.' *British Journal of Special Education*, 22(1), 12–15.

Waddington, C. (1997) 'The use of legal proceedings in cases of non-attendance at school: perceptions of education welfare officers.' *Educational Research*, 39(3), 333–41.

5 Exclusion

The number of pupils excluded from school each year is without doubt a major cause for concern. The distress that exclusion can cause both the pupil and their family is immense, and one must not be misled by the bravado displayed by some excluded pupils who claim that they are 'not bothered' by it. Exclusion implies rejection, and there is a real risk that an excluded pupil may feel that they no longer belong to the mainstream of society. Unacceptable behaviour by pupils in secondary schools which leads to an exclusion is not a new phenomenon. However, the size of the problem and the fact that a worrying number of primary school pupils are being excluded has started to sound alarm bells. The pressure on schools to raise levels of educational attainment is paradoxically contributing to exclusions, as schools often feel they now have less time to devote to coping with the needs of troublesome pupils who frequently cause problems for teachers and other pupils. As a result schools are increasingly attempting to find a formula which enables them to keep pupils at risk of exclusion 'on board' by better addressing these pupils' needs whilst at the same time not allowing such pupils to have a negative impact on the work and well-being of teachers and other pupils in the school.

What do we mean by 'school exclusion' and how common is it?

There are three categories of exclusion:

Fixed-period exclusions
A fixed-period exclusion (also known as a 'suspension') involves excluding a pupil from attending school for a fixed period, typically ranging from one to five days, although schools are required not to exclude a pupil for more than a total of 15 days in any one term.

Permanent exclusions
A permanent exclusion (also known as an 'expulsion') involves removing a pupil from the school's roll and barring them from returning. In most cases it is the LEA which is then required to arrange alternative education.

Hidden exclusions
Hidden exclusions are in effect fixed-period and permanent exclusions that have been bypassed in some way so that a formal exclusion and the need to record it as

such does not occur. An example of a 'hidden' fixed-period exclusion would be a case where a pupil is told not to return to school until some problem has been investigated and resolved, for example until they are prepared to dress according to the school's dress code. In some cases, both the school and the pupil may in fact make little effort to resolve the problem quickly, and several days may elapse before a return to school is negotiated. An example of a 'hidden' permanent exclusion would be a case where the parents are told that in the interests of the pupil they should find another school for them, and if they do not the school will permanently exclude the pupil.

Fixed-term exclusions have two major purposes. Firstly, they are used as a disciplinary sanction of last resort to help impress upon a pupil the serious level of concern about their unacceptable behaviour. Secondly, they are used to remove from the school a pupil whose behaviour is endangering their own well-being or those of others in the school.

A permanent exclusion may be used when the school feels it is unable to cope with the serious nature of the pupil's misbehaviour after a specific incident, or more usually a series of incidents. An example of a one-off incident might be selling drugs on the school premises; an example of a series of incidents might be the repeated bullying of other pupils.

The DfES (2001) guidelines on exclusions note that only a headteacher has the power to exclude a pupil from school for disciplinary reasons, and that fixed-period exclusions should normally be of short duration, unless time is needed for support to be put in place for the pupil, perhaps with assistance from the LEA. The DfES also points out that firm facts and evidence must be the basis for exclusion. This process should include an interview with the pupil facing possible exclusion. A decision to exclude a pupil should be taken only in response to serious breaches of a school's discipline policy and if allowing the pupil to stay in school would seriously harm the education or welfare of the pupil or of others in the school.

Estimating the incidence of exclusions

In the early 1990s there was a large rise in the number of permanent exclusions occurring in each year, from 2910 cases in 1990/91 to 12,668 cases in 1996/97. The figure for 2000/01 was 9210 cases, which included 92 pupils aged 5 years, 462 aged 10 years and 2484 aged 14 years. Pupils aged 14 years (the peak age for exclusions) accounted for 27 per cent of all permanently excluded pupils in 2000/01, and the rate of permanent exclusion averaged 0.04 per cent of primary school pupils and 0.27 per cent of secondary school pupils (DfES, 2002).

Vulliamy and Webb (2001) have pointed to the unreliability of the statistics gathered on exclusions at the school level, the LEA level and the national level. Detailed analyses of such statistics often reveal inconsistencies. In addition, 'hidden' or 'unofficial' exclusions contribute to the problem of measuring exclusion, for example when a pupil is forced to find another school in response to a threatened exclusion or told to remain at home for a few days as a 'cooling-off period'. A study by Stirling

(1992) indicated that the number of unofficial exclusions appears to vastly exceed the number of official exclusions.

Variations between schools

There is large variation between schools in the way that they react to what appears to be identical behaviour by pupils, which in one school leads to an exclusion but in another school does not. Vulliamy and Webb (2001) make the point that if such statistics are used to identify schools whose practice appears to be combating exclusion more successfully than others, we might in fact be learning more about school responses to target setting which enable them to avoid making officially recorded exclusions, rather than genuine success in dealing with pupils at risk of exclusion.

A study by Munn *et al.* (2001) in Scotland analysed information on 2710 excluded pupils, explored the views of 176 headteachers, and undertook case studies in eight secondary schools and four primary schools. The authors noted that schools with similar characteristics varied markedly in their exclusion rates, which they attributed to differences in the school ethos relating to the purpose of schooling, the curriculum on offer, school relations with the outside world and decision making about exclusion.

Schools are often torn between, on the one hand, trying to be sympathetic and supportive of a pupil who is clearly having major problems resulting in serious misbehaviour, and, on the other hand, the school's need to protect other pupils, staff and its own reputation from the impact of a pupil whose behaviour it is unable to control. In some cases, exclusion has been used 'in the pupil's interests' as a way of signalling the need for urgent provision to meet the pupil's special educational needs that the school felt would not be forthcoming swiftly enough through the normal procedure for assessing such needs.

Pupils at risk of exclusion

A number of studies have highlighted that pupils living in economically deprived communities, pupils living in care, pupils with statements of special educational needs and pupils from particular ethnic groups feature disproportionately more highly amongst the number of excluded pupils (Blyth and Milner, 1996; Wright *et al.*, 2000). The rate of exclusion of black Caribbean pupils has received particular attention, as it is about three times that of the national average (DfES, 2002). However, in interpreting why this group of pupils are more likely to be excluded the point has also been made that one needs to take account of the influence of risk factors such as living in deprived areas and in a family where only one parent is present, as these risk factors are also more prevalent amongst black Caribbean pupils. Nevertheless, Grant and Brooks (1996) note that a negative cycle of teachers' expectations of black Caribbean pupils may play a part in contributing to this problem.

The DfES (2001) has noted that the rate of permanent exclusion of pupils who have been statemented for their special educational needs is considerably higher than for non-statemented pupils, and advises that other than in the most exceptional circumstances, schools should avoid permanently excluding statemented pupils. Where the pupil's behaviour makes this difficult, the school should seek advice from the LEA and other professionals. If the problems remain unresolved the school should liaise with the LEA about revising the statement to provide additional support for the pupil or naming another school.

Lloyd-Smith (1993) has pointed to the wider issue that exclusion leads to a denial of the excluded pupil's entitlement to education, with a possibility that this can lead to subsequent social exclusion, disaffection, anti-social behaviour and crime that has a long-term cost for both the individual and the wider society. Consequently, whatever can be done to help schools cater for the needs of pupils at risk of exclusion can have a wider benefit for society. However, Vulliamy and Webb (2000) have argued that the government's efforts to use performance indicators of educational attainment as a means of raising standards can undermine its efforts to encourage schools to cater for pupils with a range of needs as a means of reducing social exclusion.

The picture from various studies of exclusions (Gordon, 2001; Munn *et al.*, 2001; Parsons, 1999) indicates that in general:

- the rate of exclusion in secondary schools is about nine times that of primary schools
- a quarter of secondary schools account for about two-thirds of permanent exclusions from secondary schools
- five times as many more boys are excluded as girls
- about 15 per cent of pupils who are excluded have a statement of special educational needs
- there are about four times as many fixed-period exclusions as there are permanent exclusions
- the peak rate of exclusion occurs in Year 10.

Ofsted (1996) looked at 112 cases of individual pupils with a history of indiscipline that had led to exclusion, drawn from a sample of 39 secondary schools visited. Ofsted commented that at the personal level exclusion was associated with factors such as:

- poor acquisition of basic skills, particularly literacy
- limited aspirations and opportunities
- poverty
- family difficulties
- poor relationships with other pupils, parents or teachers
- pressure from other pupils to behave in ways likely to lead to conflict with authority.

The point has often been made that many pupils face one or two problems in their personal lives without resorting to aggressive or disruptive behaviour, but that in the case of pupils excluded from school it is often evident that they face several problems in their lives. Ofsted, for example, noted that it is the combination of stresses such pupils often faced which led to a pattern of conduct characterised by:

- low attendance
- volatility and periodic aggression, sometimes interspersed with periods of cooperative behaviour
- strained relationships with adults, sometimes manifested in verbal abuse
- extreme disaffection with school, with exclusions sometimes provoked as a means of leaving school
- alcohol, drug and substance abuse
- poor mental health
- inappropriate sexual behaviour, and difficult relationships with the opposite sex
- symptoms of severe emotional disturbance, such as compulsive fire-raising or soiling
- crime.

What happens after an exclusion?

Following a permanent exclusion, an assessment is made by the LEA. Following the assessment, the pupil may then be placed in a new mainstream school, or a special school, or a pupil referral unit, or receive home tuition. Various studies have explored what happens to pupils after they have been permanently excluded from a mainstream school. The picture across these studies is mixed (Blyth and Milner, 1996; Gillborn, 1996; Imich, 1994), but overall it appears to be as follows:

- pupil referral unit: 37 per cent
- home tuition: 31 per cent
- new mainstream school: 18 per cent
- special school: 6 per cent
- exclusion reversed following an appeal: 4 per cent
- other: 4 per cent

Interestingly, a study by Kinder *et al.* (1997) based on interviews with 45 teachers, behavioural support staff and LEA officers who had been involved in exclusions indicated that they took the view that the most appropriate next stage for permanently excluded pupils was an early reintegration into mainstream education. Clearly, this is only happening in a minority of cases. Kinder *et al.* also looked at the views of 130 secondary school pupils concerning fixed-period and permanent exclusions, and made a distinction between those who 'accepted' that exclusion was a serious sanction, and experienced distress and regret in consequence, and those who 'resisted' exclusion and saw it as fun, relief or an escape. Such differing reactions to being excluded will have a major impact on whether a reintegration into mainstream is likely to be successful.

In general, pupils in primary school are twice as likely to move to another mainstream school (28 per cent) than is the case for pupils in secondary schools (14 per cent). This is because the proportion of pupils who are permanently excluded is highest towards the end of compulsory schooling, and for these older pupils there is not enough time to arrange for the possibility of moving to another school (either a mainstream or a special school); the parents and pupils are often much less cooperative; and the presenting problems are often much more serious (e.g. drug trafficking or assaulting a teacher). The procedures to be followed by a school that lead to a permanent exclusion are covered by various pieces of legislation, and the right to appeal against such a decision also exists, with successful appeals often based on the grounds that the proper procedures have not been followed (Cooke and Gregory, 2001; Gillborn, 1996). In 2000/01 27 per cent of the appeals which were lodged were decided in the parents' favour (DfES, 2002). The final category of 'other' is an estimate of the number of cases where no provision appears to have been made. In some cases these pupils are very near to the end of Year 11, or may have left the LEA and tracing what has happened to them may be very difficult.

Exclusion from primary schools

Although exclusions are much less common in primary schools, the fact that many pupils are being excluded at such a young age is a major cause for concern (Hayden, 1997; Hayden *et al.*, 1996). Hayden (1994) argues that excluding a primary school pupil can be much more damaging than for a secondary school pupil, in that the pupil will be missing out not only on the development of essential skills of numeracy and literacy but also on the development of their social skills through daily contact with their peers and responsible adults outside their immediate family and local community.

What are the main causes of and reasons for school exclusions?

Mitchell (1998) has reported that the most frequent precipitating incidents cited by schools fall into five categories:

- *violence*, including assaults on children, teachers and other adults
- *disruption*, including disruption in lessons, refusal to accept punishments, breaking contracts, and misbehaviour which disrupts the smooth running of the school
- *verbal abuse*, including insolence, swearing and disobedience to staff, and abusive language to other pupils
- *criminal behaviour*, including drug-related activities, vandalism and theft
- *truancy*, plus other attendance problems including absconding.

Studies of the causes of exclusion (Imich, 1994; Gordon, 2001; Munn *et al.*, 2001) indicate that violence accounts for about 35 per cent of cases of exclusion, followed by disruption (28 per cent), verbal abuse (22 per cent), criminal behaviour (10 per cent) and truancy (5 per cent).

Given that most exclusions occur as a result of violent and disruptive behaviour, the main causes of exclusion can be seen to lie in the interaction between, on the one hand, factors in the pupil's home and community environment that predispose them to behave in a violent and disruptive way at school and, on the other hand, factors in the school environment that act as the 'trigger' for such behaviour. For such pupils, there are four types of situation that are likely to trigger serious disruptive behaviour. These are situations based on their perception that:

- the teacher is boring
- the teacher continually gives them work which is too difficult and will not help them
- the teacher makes unfair personal remarks about them
- the teacher acts in a hostile way towards them.

For pupils who have a 'short fuse' the level of frustration that can build up in these situations means that any interaction whereby the teacher tries to coerce the pupil to get on with the work can precipitate a confrontation in which the pupil behaves in a way that the teacher finds totally unacceptable. Skilful teaching that enables pupils to stay on task and that can quickly and smoothly defuse any conflict will do much to minimise serious misbehaviour. In one important sense, then, one cause of exclusion is that some teachers simply lack the skills needed to keep such pupils on task. However, it is worth bearing in mind that there clearly has to be a limit to what we can expect of a teacher in this respect, since attempting to keep some pupils on task may involve spending an unfairly disproportionate amount of time on their needs at the expense of others in the class and, to some extent, tolerating a level of misbehaviour that interferes from time to time with the smooth running of a lesson.

Disruptive behaviour

The Elton Report (DES, 1989) on discipline in schools noted that pupils who were most at risk of engaging in persistent disruptive behaviour were those who had a highly stressed family background and a history of poor achievement at school. Such pupils are likely to have low self-esteem and to express their frustration through aggression. The Elton Report concluded that much could be done to reduce persistent serious misbehaviour in schools by upgrading teachers' skills to deal with particularly challenging pupils. The report also noted the range of misbehaviour that occurs in schools which teachers need to deal with (see Table 5.1), based on a questionnaire completed by 1083 primary and 2525 secondary school teachers in England and Wales. This reminds us that in deploying the time, energy and skill needed to deal effectively with a pupil who is particularly challenging, teachers are acting against a backdrop of misbehaviour by other pupils which, although less challenging and not placing them in any danger of exclusion, also needs to be dealt with effectively.

A number of studies have also highlighted the extent to which exclusion rates vary between schools that appear to have a similar intake of pupils. This would seem to indicate that some schools are either more successful than others in handling challenging pupils or more tolerant of the level of misbehaviour that they are

Table 5.1 Frequency of pupil misbehaviour reported by teachers as occurring during lessons at least daily

Type of pupil misbehaviour	Reported by primary teachers (%)	Reported by secondary teachers (%)
Talking out of turn (e.g. by making remarks, calling out, distracting others by chattering)	69	53
Hindering other pupils (e.g. by distracting them from work, interfering with equipment or materials)	42	26
Making unnecessary (non-verbal) noise (e.g. by scraping chairs, banging objects, moving clumsily)	42	25
Getting out of seat without permission	34	14
Calculated idleness or work avoidance (e.g. delaying start to work set, not having essential books or equipment)	21	25
Persistently infringing class (or school) rules (e.g. on dress, pupil behaviour)	13	17
Not being punctual (e.g. being late to school or lessons)	11	17
General rowdiness, horseplay or mucking about	14	10
Physical aggression towards other pupils (e.g. pushing, punching, striking)	17	6
Verbal abuse towards other pupils (e.g. offensive or insulting remarks)	10	10
Cheeky or impertinent remarks or responses	6	10
Physical destructiveness (e.g. breaking objects, damaging furniture and fabric)	1	1
Verbal abuse towards the teacher (e.g. offensive, insulting, insolent or threatening remarks)	1	1
Physical aggression towards the teacher	0	0

Source: DES (1989)

prepared to accommodate before resorting to exclusion. Research on school differences in exclusion rates suggests that both these factors are in operation.

For example, the Social Exclusion Unit (1998) noted that the reasons given for exclusion by schools fell into three categories:

- incidents that are relatively minor and were never meant to be grounds for exclusion
- more serious incidents, which with the right support could be prevented from arising or could be tackled in schools, without the draconian sanction of exclusion
- a final category of serious, possibly criminal, incidents where exclusion is fully justified.

The Unit noted that far too many cases of permanent exclusion fell into the first two categories, and as such should be avoidable. It pointed to the official guidance on exclusions (DFE, 1994) which says that exclusion should only be used in response to serious breaches of a school's policy on behaviour or of criminal law, and as a last resort when all other reasonable steps have been taken and when allowing the pupil to remain in school would be seriously detrimental to the education or welfare of that pupil or others. Nevertheless, it also noted that some schools are so anxious to avoid exclusions that they incur some danger to staff and pupils.

Factors influencing whether to exclude

The DFE (1994) guidelines on exclusion also list factors that the headteacher should take into account in deciding whether to exclude. These include:

- mitigating circumstances such as a strained or traumatic domestic situation
- whether or not the behaviour impaired or will impair the normal functioning of the pupil or other pupils in the school
- the extent to which parental, peer or other pressure may have contributed to the behaviour
- whether the incident was perpetrated by the pupil on their own or as part of a group
- the degree to which the behaviour was a violation of one or more rules contained in the school's policy on behaviour.

The extent to which each of these factors is susceptible to different interpretations and will be weighed differently at different schools will also contribute to the variation in rates of exclusion between schools.

The DFE guidance also emphasises the importance of ensuring that a permanent exclusion occurs only after all other reasonable steps have been taken. These reasonable prior steps would include:

- alternative sanctions
- interviewing the pupil and parents

- identifying special educational needs
- negotiating agreements with the pupil and parent
- issuing a formal warning
- withdrawing from class
- involving social services or the police.

What can schools do to help pupils 'at risk' of exclusion and reduce exclusions?

Gordon (2001) has emphasised the need to take account of the views of excluded pupils themselves if we are to understand why some who are at risk of exclusion are eventually excluded. There is little doubt that the persistent misbehaviour of some pupils, despite help, warnings and fixed-period exclusions, indicates a degree of frustration and disaffection that schools simply are unable to deal with and for which a permanent exclusion becomes almost inevitable. Intervention strategies need to target pupils as early as possible once a cause for concern has been identified, in order to stem the development of disaffection.

Blyth and Milner (1994) have argued that to combat exclusion we have to go beyond 'victim blaming', which essentially views exclusion as the result of the inability of schools to manage the challenging behaviour of certain pupils. They argue that we need rather to understand the complex tension between, on the one hand, pupils' views of themselves, their aspirations, their view of job opportunities and what schools have to offer and, on the other hand, the way schools operate to provide mass education within a framework of academic demands set down by the state education system. Underlying the incidents which result in exclusion are pupils with low self-esteem and low attainment, who become increasingly frustrated, disaffected and alienated from what schools have to offer. Combating exclusion needs to deal effectively with these underlying causes as much as with the presenting incidents.

Reducing exclusions

Ofsted (1996) identified five factors which were crucial in influencing a school's success in reducing exclusions:

- the effectiveness of the school behaviour policy
- the application of suitable rewards and sanctions
- the effectiveness of strategies to monitor exclusion
- the quality of pastoral support
- the extent of curriculum modification.

Overall, there are two main approaches that a school needs to follow to minimise exclusions. The first approach is to minimise pupil disaffection. The pupil most at risk of exclusion is one who has low self-esteem, finds the work that is demanded too difficult, and feels that the curriculum offered has little relevance to their lives.

Such pupils become disaffected, bored and frustrated. Persistent misbehaviour is in large measure for them a response to their frustration and an attempt to protect their self-esteem from exposure to persistent academic failure. Action that can be taken to minimise disaffection includes attractive curricular and non-curricular activities, feedback from teachers which can help raise the pupils' self-esteem, remedial support for pupils in basic skills, and a flexible curriculum that can include areas in which the pupil can achieve success and which they feel are relevant to their needs. Schemes such as offering older pupils or adults as mentors to at-risk pupils can help here. Gordon (2001) makes the point that we need more research to look at the views of excluded pupils themselves in order to explore what strategies might effectively motivate disaffected pupils.

The second approach is to minimise the extent to which misbehaviour needs to be referred to the headteacher. All schools have a hierarchical management structure which can broadly be grouped into three levels for small schools: the classroom teacher, middle management and the headteacher; and into four levels for large schools: the classroom teacher, middle management, senior management and the headteacher. In schools where most incidents of misbehaviour can be dealt with effectively by the classroom teacher and middle management, the likelihood of exclusion is much reduced. However, in schools where such incidents are very quickly referred to the headteacher to deal with, the risk of exclusion becomes much greater. This speed of upward referral is a critical feature in explaining differences in exclusion rates between schools which serve a very similar catchment. This difference is not simply a matter of whether one school has teachers who are better skilled in dealing with misbehaviour. Rather, it largely reflects the ethos and priorities of the school. Dealing with persistent misbehaviour by a pupil takes time, effort and energy, and more resources devoted to such pupils means less resources devoted to meeting the needs of other pupils in the school. All schools need to decide how much of their time, energy and effort can fairly be devoted to pupils who persistently misbehave. In schools where teachers and middle mangers feel that the ethos of the school dictates that relatively little time should be devoted to such pupils, these pupils are likely to be speedily referred upwards, become drawn to the headteacher's attention, and if the misbehaviour persists, are then likely to be excluded.

Action that can be taken to reduce the speed of upward referral is thus very important in minimising the need for exclusion. This means that classroom teachers in particular need to be skilled in the techniques which minimise and defuse potential confrontation in the classroom, and middle managers need to be able to apply counselling skills and supportive coercion to help pupils cope with the demands being made upon them.

The impact of pressure on schools to raise attainment

In the early 1990s the use of league tables based on pupil attainment led many schools to believe the government's agenda was to prioritise the drive to raise academic standards, and in response to this schools devoted less time, energy and effort to pupils who persistently misbehaved, which had the effect of producing a marked rise in the rate of exclusions.

In the study by Munn *et al.* (2001) referred to earlier, the authors noted that schools which discouraged exclusion valued both social and academic goals; offered a lively informal curriculum which included sport, art and working in the local community; involved parents in decision making about their children; and used behaviour and learning support staff to help and advise mainstream staff rather than simply to take troublesome pupils. In addition, a study by Mitchell (1998) has indicated that the headteacher's philosophy regarding the extent to which the needs of a minority of pupils who persistently misbehaved should be balanced against those of the majority has a crucial impact on the school culture in relation to upward referral.

Inter-agency cooperation

A number of studies have highlighted the important role that needs to be played by inter-agency cooperation both in supporting pupils and schools when a pupil is at risk of exclusion and in helping to support a pupil returning to school after a fixed-period exclusion or moving to a new school after a permanent exclusion. For example, Hayden (1994) looked at the use of an inter-agency group under the lead role of social services to help 12 boys aged 6 to 10 years identified by five primary schools as having behaviour problems. It was clear that the records on each pupil held by the different agencies (social services, the police, the schools) when looked at together provided a much richer insight into the nature of each pupil's problems, circumstances and needs than the school had access to when working alone.

A study by Normington and Kyriacou (1994) focused on the interdisciplinary work that occurs following permanent exclusion for a sample of excluded pupils based at a pupil referral unit. This study interviewed the professionals concerned, which included educational psychologists, education welfare officers, peripatetic support workers, and teachers. They reported that the quality of such inter-agency cooperation is often hampered by heavy case loads and by difficulties in the different agencies keeping each other fully informed, and as such is an area that needs better resources.

A study by Vulliamy and Webb (1999) reported that a project which involved five full-time school-based home–school support workers working in seven secondary schools in York and North Yorkshire had a considerable impact on reducing fixed-period and permanent exclusions. The support workers worked with 157 pupils identified by the school for inclusion in the project. Most of these pupils had been involved in disrupting lessons, had attendance problems and had offended. About half of the pupils in the caseload were in Years 9 and 10. The support workers were able to address the problems facing these pupils in the following ways:

- befriending
- offering ongoing counselling and support
- using individual approaches and group work to improve, for example, anger management, self-esteem and relationships with peers

- advocacy and mediation between pupils, peers, teachers and parents/carers
- identifying out-of-school leisure activities and facilitating participation
- advising on personal, social and health problems
- referral to other agencies.

Of particular interest in the success of this project was the way in which the parents and pupils were willing to accept and respond positively to the role of the support workers in helping the pupils mitigate behaviour that would have placed them at risk of exclusion. This study also indicated that such support workers can play a key role in improving the quality of the inter-agency cooperation (Webb and Vulliamy, 2001).

Working with pupils and parents

Working with pupils and parents is particularly crucial in the period following a fixed-period exclusion. The DfES (2001) has pointed out that although headteachers are not legally bound to consult the parents before excluding a pupil, the parents and pupil should be warned in advance if exclusion becomes a likely prospect. Once a pupil is excluded, headteachers must notify the parents immediately, ideally by telephone. This should be followed up at once by a letter, setting out the exclusion for the fixed period, and the date and time when the pupil should return. Work should be provided for any pupil who is excluded for longer than one school day. Schools should ensure that this work is marked and that further work is set until the pupil returns to school. The contact between the school and the pupil and parents during this period can help indicate that the school is doing its best to ensure that the pupil learns from this experience and is able to return and reintegrate successfully.

In addition, some schools will ask the pupil to sign a *re-admittance contract*, which is sometimes also signed by the headteacher and parents. In the contract, the pupil agrees to behave in certain ways in the future. For example, one contract listed the following three conditions:

- I will behave well at all times.
- I will be polite to staff and pupils.
- I will complete all homework and lesson work.

Such contracts help to reinforce in the pupil's mind the seriousness of the situation in which they find themselves and thereby help them to agree in a determined way to improve their behaviour. However, it is essential that whatever conditions are agreed to must be realistic, particularly as pupils will be tempted to agree to anything without really feeling a commitment to abide by what they have signed. Consequently the contract needs to be talked through with them. The pupil should be asked to propose what behaviour they need to improve and this is then negotiated with the school until certain behaviours are agreed. The process of drawing up the contract provides a real opportunity to change the pupil's mindset, and it is this process that is of key importance rather than what is actually written, particularly as what is written will often appear to be rather general, as in the above example.

Emotional and behavioural difficulties

Where serious and persistent misbehaviour occurs, the pupil may need to be assessed to ascertain whether they have special needs as a result of *emotional and behavioural difficulties* (EBD), for which additional support and provision may be made either in school or by placement in a special school. A distinction needs to be made between emotional difficulties and behavioural difficulties. The former relates to emotional problems, such as anxieties, phobias, depression and extreme withdrawal, which in extreme cases may constitute a psychiatrically diagnosed emotional disorder, such as depression. The latter relates to behavioural problems, such as anti-social behaviour, truancy, stealing and violence towards others, which in extreme cases may constitute as psychiatrically diagnosed conduct disorder. Such pupils are at high risk of exclusion.

Behaviour modification

Much has been written about the action that schools can take to minimise the need to exclude pupils (Cooper *et al.*, 2000; McSherry, 2001; Munn *et al.*, 2000). Of particular interest has been the use of *behaviour modification strategies* to enable particularly challenging pupils to modify and control their behaviour.

Behaviour modification involves the use of principles derived from behavioural psychology to bring about improved behaviour in the classroom. This 'behavioural approach' is based on the notion that behaviour which is followed by reward is reinforced and as such is more likely to occur in the same circumstances in the future, whereas behaviour which is not rewarded (i.e. is ignored or punished) is less likely to reoccur. This approach has been used in both primary schools and secondary schools to target particular pupils and classes whose behaviour gives cause for concern.

The use of behaviour modification in the classroom usually involves a period in which the level of some desirable and undesirable behaviours is recorded (e.g. amount of time spent out of seat, amount of time spent working, number of times pupil disrupts another pupil). These are termed the 'target behaviours'. Sometimes the programme is directed at improving the behaviour of one particular pupil, whilst on other occasions it is intended to improve the behaviour of the whole class. In both cases, a treatment phase is then implemented in which instances of the desirable behaviours by the target pupil (or pupils) are systematically rewarded (e.g. by use of praise, or award of tokens to be redeemed later for sweets or other rewards), and instances of undesirable behaviours are ignored (these instances are generally ignored rather than punished). Once behaviour has improved, the level of frequency of the rewards is gradually reduced. Finally, a post-treatment phase is used to monitor the level of the desirable and undesirable behaviours in order to verify whether the treatment has been successful and also to help establish what level of reward needs to employed in future to maintain the desirable behaviours. The key to behaviour modification in the classroom thus lies in the following:

- careful monitoring of the target behaviours
- systematic and consistent reward of the desirable behaviours
- ignoring undesirable behaviours.

The use of behaviour modification contrasts with the approach to discipline of most teachers, who tend to concentrate on reprimanding and punishing undesirable behaviours and rarely commenting on or explicitly rewarding good behaviour. The idea of ignoring undesirable behaviour would be regarded by most teachers as suspect and unworkable. 'Behaviourists' argue, however, that much misbehaviour is simply a form of attention seeking, and as such, if it is ignored pupils quickly switch to the desirable behaviour which gains the teacher's attention and praise.

One major feature of the use of behaviour modification in schools is that the pupils are often told explicitly in a prior discussion of the need to engage in the desirable behaviours and agree to the type of rewards that will follow sustained desirable behaviours. The desirable behaviours may be stated in terms of adherence to classroom rules such as the following:

- We stay in our seats whilst working.
- We get on with our work quietly.
- We try not to interrupt.

The pupils are thus well aware that they are being monitored and what rewards will follow. Indeed, this is often set up as a type of game, and in some cases groups of pupils sitting at different desks in the classroom may compete with each other to see which group is best behaved and will get the best reward. In these cases peer pressure is then used by pupils against a pupil in the group who starts misbehaving.

Promoting inclusion

Action taken to reduce truancy can also have a big impact on reducing exclusion as it can help prevent a downward spiral in behaviour and attainment. Better attendance will also mean that the pupil is less likely to find they have missed the work that is needed to cope with the academic demands made on them.

Another route for schools is to draw up a *pastoral support plan* for any pupil at risk of exclusion. This plan is tailored to meet the needs of the pupil, and enables the pupil and school to reach an agreement on how the school can help the pupil to behave appropriately in future. The plan will typically consider:

- the pupils' learning difficulties, particularly literacy and numeracy skills, putting in place a remedial programme and access forms of study support such as lunchtime and after-school homework clubs
- disapplying the National Curriculum
- changing the pupil's teaching set or class, which could enable the pupil to work with

a teacher better able to meet their needs and could also include using a mentor or buddy to work alongside the pupil

- attaching the pupil to a personal adviser from the Connexions service
- jointly registering the pupil with a pupil referral unit to benefit from the unit's expertise while remaining at the school
- drawing up an agreement with parents on their role
- transfer to another school to offer a fresh start
- arranging specialist support and counselling, such as for a bereavement or drug dependency
- spending some time in an inclusion unit.

An *inclusion unit* is a specific unit on the school site where troubled pupils, often at risk of exclusion, can have their individual needs met. These units are designed to ensure that pupils who are having problems and causing disruption in the normal classroom setting are able to continue their education. The main aim of these units is to reintegrate pupils into normal schooling as soon as possible, rather than to offer an alternative education. The minimum time that is spent is such units is usually two weeks and the maximum time is usually six weeks. During their time in this unit, pupils' needs are met in a number of ways. These include:

- the use of specialised teachers
- small teaching groups
- social skills development activities (e.g. anger management, enhancing self-esteem)
- a short-term rewards system
- enrichment activities to get them interested in learning
- an emphasis on learning in key subject areas (English, mathematics and science).

In some secondary schools, the inclusion unit is targeted at pupils in Key Stage 3, where it is felt the school's investment in time and effort is most likely to have positive outcomes. For example, one school handbook describes its inclusion unit as a facility for a small and varying clientele of pupils in Years 7 and 8 who present the following problems:

- For a variety of reasons they are not managing to cope in some lessons.
- They have returned from a lengthy illness.
- They have returned from a fixed-period exclusion.
- They find it very difficult to concentrate, cannot ignore distractions and lack self-control.
- They suffer from school phobia.
- They have personal and social problems that require a short-term response.

The pupils attending the inclusion unit should wherever possible cover the same work as their peers to allow for their reintegration.

Good behaviour policies

These involve encouraging pupils to behave well by having a system of encouragements and rewards in place that support, acknowledge and praise good behaviour. The emphasis here is on getting pupils to think about the importance of behaving well and the need to contribute to the establishment of a positive school ethos. Such policies deal as much with supporting good behaviour as they do with dealing with misbehaviour. In terms of dealing with misbehaviour, the emphasis is on supporting the pupil to understand the need to behave well in future and supporting their efforts to do this, rather than taking a harsh and draconian response to misbehaviour which can simply serve to alienate the pupil from the school.

Remedial support for basic skills

Such support seeks to enable pupils to cope with the academic work that faces them and to prevent them becoming frustrated and disaffected by their failure to engage with the lesson demands made upon them. The success of this approach relies heavily on the early identification of such needs, and an awareness that some pupils may seek to mask their needs by appearing to be lazy or uninterested in the work rather than admit to having basic problems with literacy and numeracy. Remedial help also needs to be offered with sensitivity so that such pupils do not feel they are being labelled by teachers and peers in a derogatory manner.

Inclusion units

The use of an on-site inclusion unit for troubled pupils can allow such pupils a period of time in which to continue their education outside the normal classroom setting, after which they can be reintegrated. This time can sometimes be used flexibly, to allow for a pupil who is having problems in a particular subject area or with a particular teacher to go to the inclusion unit for those particular lessons so that time can be made available in which the problems can be sorted out. It is usual, however, to require a minimum time of about two weeks to be spent in such a unit, so that the unit does not turn into a 'sin bin' used for one-off lessons, but rather is seen to provide a coherent programme of support for the pupil. A maximum time also helps to ensure that the pupils do not become attached to and dependent on the staff at the unit and the more individual nature of the attention provided there, which, if continued for too long, could make reintegration difficult.

Behaviour modification

Behaviour modification schemes can provide a useful framework to help pupils to modify and control their behaviour. A number of schemes have

been targeted at pupils who have emotional and behavioural difficulties and have proved to be successful in helping them to avoid exclusion.

Adaptable curriculum

All pupils need to engage in activities in school in which they can experience success and which they feel are relevant and worthwhile. For pupils who experience difficulties in the core academic curriculum, activities such as drama, art, music, sports, community service, outward bound events and outside visits can provide opportunities that increase self-confidence and self-esteem. A flexible approach to the academic curriculum can also allow many academic tasks to be accessed in a more user-friendly manner by pupils who find a dry academic emphasis difficult to cope with. In addition, the curriculum can include courses which have a stronger vocational relevance to pupils. Such courses can offer an important 'new start' or 'second chance' to pupils who have experienced repeated failure in traditional academic subjects. The use of youth award schemes and other certificated programmes that offer success for participation in a variety of challenging tasks can play a part here.

Slowing down upward referral

Classroom teachers who are skilled at dealing with challenging behaviour and disaffection are often able to cope with and indeed win over pupils who might otherwise need to be referred upwards to a more senior member of staff in the school for persistent misbehaviour. Upward referral will also be lessened if classroom teachers know that additional support is available to them in the form of the school's support systems, which may be able to provide additional resources to meet the pupils' educational needs or provide a 'cooling-off' room where disruptive pupils can be sent from time to time if their behaviour becomes unacceptable. The efforts of the classroom teacher to deal with difficult pupils in this way need to be supported by the school ethos and consistent with the actions of other staff in the school.

Pastoral support

The quality of pastoral care is key to supporting pupils whose behaviour is giving cause for concern. Most exclusions occur after a period of misbehaviour rather than following a one-off incident. Successful intervention to combat disaffection is therefore crucial. Many excluded pupils feel that the school did not really understand their problems or help them to overcome them. Whilst these feelings may often be unfair, it is clear that a pupil's perception of the degree of help they are getting is crucial to their sense of being part of the school community and hence their efforts to behave acceptably. The support of parents and the involvement of outside agencies are important here, and skilful pastoral

care staff can often engage parents' cooperation even in difficult circumstances. Some schools offer a pastoral support plan drawn up after consultation between the school, parents and other agencies to pupils at risk of exclusion in which a series of short-term targets covering three or four months can be set and assessed.

Counselling

Some pupils need help to develop social skills that will enable them to cope with their frustrations. Anger management training in particular can be very helpful. Some pupils need to be helped to develop self-insight and to understand the need to act in their own best interests by confronting and seeking help for problems in appropriate ways. Some pupils may need help to withstand coercion from peers to misbehave. Low self-esteem is common amongst pupils at risk of exclusion, and in some cases they need to be helped to understand that many of the circumstances they face are not of their own making and that they should not feel that these should undermine their feelings about their own sense of worth.

Mentoring

Some schemes have been set up in which older pupils and adults can act as a mentor for pupils who persistently misbehave, in order to support and encourage their efforts to behave better in future. This 'older brother/sister' acts as a point of reference, confidant or role model for pupils who might respond well to a longer term positive influence of this sort to counteract the negative influence they may be receiving from others.

Social workers

Various schemes have shown that the use of full-time social workers or home–school support workers attached to a group of schools can play a role in mediating between the school, the parents and outside agencies, so that the help and support that the pupil receives is well informed, coordinated and appropriate to the problem. In addition, social workers can provide both parents and teachers with further information and support so that they can play their part more effectively. Social workers are also often seen by parents and pupils as being very supportive, and hence are less likely to engender a defensive and non-cooperative reaction compared with the response they may give to approaches from teachers.

Inter-agency cooperation

A number of studies have highlighted the important role that needs to be played by inter-agency cooperation, both before and after an exclusion has occurred. In many cases, the circumstances that a pupil faces are

extremely serious and complex. These may include abuse at home, serious criminal activity, and drug abuse. In such cases, inter-agency cooperation is crucial for the precise circumstances involved in the case to be unravelled, and for action to be coordinated. In some cases, the pupil may be in physical danger or in need of urgent medical attention. In other cases, with appropriate support from outside agencies, a return to mainstream school can be successful. This may take the form of a partial return to the school in the first instance with other types of support being made available to the pupil to address their home circumstances.

Help after an exclusion

Successful reintegration to a mainstream school following a fixed period or permanent exclusion needs to be well planned, carefully monitored and well supported. In particular, the pupil needs to be made aware of both what is expected from their behaviour and the nature of the help that will be provided to assist with their reintegration. It is crucial here that the pupil is clear about which member of the school staff will be monitoring their reintegration and that they feel confident that they can approach this teacher for help and advice if any problems arise, so that problems are recognised and dealt with at an early stage rather than ignored and thereby allowed to fester and develop further.

Working with excluded pupils and their parents

Enlisting the help and support of parents and the pupil following an exclusion can be crucial to the success of what follows. Some parents may well have been troubled by their child's behaviour themselves, and may see an exclusion as an opportunity to get help and support from the school and other agencies. Similarly, some pupils may feel their problems arise from their parents' behaviour or other aspects of their home circumstances, and they too may see an exclusion as an opportunity to get help and support. Work with the parents and the excluded pupil needs to carefully identify and address the underlying causes for the problem behaviour that gave rise to the exclusion, and to identify what action can be taken in cooperation with the parents and the pupil to lead to positive outcomes.

References

Blyth, E. and Milner, J. (1994) 'Exclusion from school and victim-blaming.' *Oxford Review of Education*, 20(3), 293–306.

Blyth, E. and Milner, J. (eds) (1996) *Exclusion from School: Inter-Professional Issues for Policy and Practice*. London: Routledge.

Cooke, R. and Gregory, I. (2001) *Exclusion and the Law: A Guide for Headteachers and Governors.* Nafferton: Studies in Education.

Cooper, P., Drummond, M. D., Hart, S., Lovey, J. and McLaughlin, C. (2000) *Positive Alternatives to Exclusion.* London: RoutledgeFalmer.

DES (1989) *Discipline in Schools (The Elton Report).* London: HMSO.

DFE (1994) *Exclusions from School. DFE Circular 10/94.* London: DFE.

DfES (2001) *Exclusions.* DfES website: www.dfes.gov.uk/a-z/atozindex.html.

DfES (2002) *Exclusions 2000/01.* DfES website: www.dfes.gov.uk.

Gillborn, D. (1996) *Exclusions from School. Viewpoint No. 5.* London: University of London Institute of Education.

Gordon, A. (2001) 'School exclusions in England: children's voices and adult solutions?' *Educational Studies*, 27(1), 69–85.

Grant, D. and Brooks, K. (1996) 'Exclusion from school: responses from the black community.' *Pastoral Care in Education*, 14(3), 20–7.

Hayden, C. (1994) 'Primary age children excluded from school: a multi-agency focus for concern.' *Children and Society*, 8(3), 257–73.

Hayden, C. (1997) *Children Excluded from Primary School: Debates, Evidence, Responses.* Buckingham: Open University Press.

Hayden, C., Sheppard, C. and Ward, D. (1996) 'Primary exclusions: evidence for action.' *Educational Research*, 38(2), 213–25.

Imich, A. J. (1994) 'Exclusions from school: current trends and issues.' *Educational Research*, 36(1), 3–11.

Kinder, K., Wilkin, A. and Wakefield, A. (1997) *Exclusion: Who Needs It?* Slough: NFER.

Lloyd-Smith, M. (1993) 'Problem behaviour, exclusions and the policy vacuum.' *Pastoral Care in Education*, 11(4), 19–24.

McSherry, J. (2001) *Challenging Behaviours in Mainstream Schools: Practical Strategies for Effective Intervention and Reintegration.* London: David Fulton.

Mitchell, L. (1998) *Naughty or Needy? Exclusions: A Study of One Local Education Authority.* DPhil thesis, University of York.

Munn, P., Lloyd, G. and Cullen, M. A. (2000) *Alternatives to Exclusion from School.* London: Paul Chapman.

Munn, P., Cullen, M. A., Johnstone, M. and Lloyd, G. (2001) 'Exclusion from school: a view from Scotland on policy and practice.' *Research Papers in Education*, 16(1), 23–42.

Normington, J. and Kyriacou, C. (1994) 'Exclusion from high schools and the work of the outside agencies involved.' *Pastoral Care in Education*,12(4), 12–15.

Ofsted (1996) *Exclusions from Secondary Schools 1995/96.* London: The Stationery Office.

Parsons, C. (1999) *Education, Exclusion and Citizenship.* London: Routledge.

Social Exclusion Unit (1998) *Truancy and School Exclusion.* London: The Stationery Office.

Stirling, M. (1992) 'How many pupils are being excluded?' *British Journal of Special Education*, 19(4), 128–30.

Vulliamy, G. and Webb, R. (1999) *Meeting Need and Challenging Crime in Partnership with Schools, Research Findings No. 96.* London: Home Office Research, Development and Statistics Directorate.

Vulliamy, G. and Webb, R. (2000) 'Stemming the tide of rising school exclusions: problems and possibilities.' *British Journal of Educational Studies*, 48(2), 119–33.

Vulliamy, G. and Webb, R. (2001) 'The social construction of school exclusion rates: implications for evaluation methodology.' *Educational Studies*, 27(3), 357–70.

Webb, R. and Vulliamy, G. (2001) 'Joining up the solutions: the rhetoric and practice of inter-agency cooperation.' *Children and Society*, 15(4), 315–32.

Wright, C., Weekes, D. and McGlaughlin, A. (2000) *'Race', Class and Gender in Exclusion from School.* London: Falmer Press.

6   Stress

There is little doubt that the academic demands that schools make on pupils can generate anxieties and fears from time to time. It is well accepted that the period leading to important examinations can certainly generate a great deal of stress. However, there are many other aspects of schooling that can upset pupils. These include being reprimanded by a teacher, finding the work too difficult, and adjusting to a new social and organisational environment. For some pupils, the level of stress generated by such situations can affect their mental and physical health. It has been increasingly recognised that almost all pupils need to develop effective coping strategies to deal with the stress they experience at school, and that some pupils need substantial help, support and counselling in order to cope with the pressures and worries they experience.

What do we mean by 'pupil stress' and how common is it?

Pupil stress can be defined as the experience by pupils of negative emotions such as anxiety, anger, depression and frustration resulting from some aspect of schooling. The term focuses on the stress generated by being a pupil in a school, and needs to be distinguished from other sources of stress a pupil may experience which are generated outside school, such as an aspect of life at home (e.g. worries about parents who argue all the time) or personal matters (e.g. a long-term illness). Of course, stress generated outside school can impact on a pupil's mood and behaviour while they are at school, but it should not be regarded as a source of pupil stress. Pupil stress deals specifically with the worries and concerns experienced by pupils which are generated by some aspect of their role as a pupil and the demands made upon them by schools.

Estimating the incidence of pupil stress

The extent of pupil stress can be estimated from studies which have used questionnaires and interviews to explore how frequently pupils worry about their experiences at school. These indicate that stress is a common phenomenon at school and that almost all pupils will experience some stress from time to time in a typical week. However, for some pupils their circumstances are such that they will experience a high level of stress on a regular basis. This might be common in pupils who are continually finding the work too difficult and become frustrated and depressed by this experience. In addition, some pupils will experience a high level of stress at particular times, such as in the run-up to some important examination, or after falling out with a group of friends.

The frequency of stress depends to some extent on the context in which the pupil is working, for example if they have parents who are putting immense pressure on them to achieve at a level which is beyond their capabilities. In addition, some pupils appear to be more stress-prone than others, such as those who have a personality predisposition to be anxious or those who have a low self-esteem and are inclined to blame themselves for anything that goes wrong.

Overall, our best estimate is that about 10 per cent of pupils experience a high level of pupil stress as indicated by self-report measures of their feelings about school (concerns, anxieties, worries and depression) and by stress-related symptoms, such as feeling sick, or having aches and pains that they attribute to aspects of their school experience.

A study by Bru *et al.* (1998) explored pupil stress amongst 1071 secondary school pupils aged 15 years in Norway, and found that about 12 per cent of this sample reported stress-related emotional complaints and about 10 per cent reported stress-related musculoskeletal complaints. The incidence of such complaints was highest for pupils who had learning difficulties and for pupils who were frequently being bullied.

The proportion of pupils who experience high levels of stress may, however, increase sharply at times of particular pressure, such as in the run-up to important examinations. For example, a study by Hodge *et al.* (1997) looked at the stress levels of 445 pupils aged 16 to 18 years in New South Wales, Australia, who were studying for their Higher School Certificate examinations (the equivalent of A levels in England). The students completed the General Health Questionnaire, which is used to identify people whose mental health is 'at risk'. Over half of the pupils in this study had scores which were above the cut-off point for being at risk, and these scores were greater for those nearer to the examinations.

In addition, there are extreme events, albeit rare, that can occur at school or during school trips which can be traumatising for all those involved, such as accidents resulting in the serious injury or death of a pupil or teacher, serious fires, serious assaults, robbery and rape (Kinchin and Brown, 2001; Sharp and Cowie, 1998), and guidelines have been produced to help advise schools on what to do after such traumatic events have occurred to offer help and counselling to those involved (Shears, 1995; Yule and Gold, 1993).

The signs of stress

Mills (1992) has listed physical and behavioural signs and symptoms that will enable a teacher to identify a pupil experiencing stress overload:

- *physical:* muscular aches and pains, darkness around eyes, diarrhoea, pale colour, sickness, skin rashes, frequent visits to toilet, signs of tension in face, difficulty in swallowing, self-mutilation, sore eyes, cold sores, headaches, loss or gain in weight, frequent coughs and colds, bruising and burns

- *behavioural:* becoming isolated, picking arguments, tearfulness, angry outbursts, work not up to date, carelessness/mistakes/untidiness, bullying other children, staring out of window and daydreaming, poor concentration, giving up easily, sarcasm; seeking attention, lack of care with appearance, loss of sense of humour.

The stress process

Studies of the stress process indicate that the key factor in a person's experience of stress is the perception of threat. There are many aspects of a pupil's environment that can be a potential source of stress (a potential stressor). These include examinations, falling out with friends and getting critical feedback from a teacher about one's work. What turns a 'potential stressor' into an 'actual stressor' is the pupil's perception that the situation threatens their self-esteem or well-being in some way. Stress is the body's natural response to danger. In evolutionary terms, it is the physiological mechanism that has evolved to prepare us for 'fight' or 'flight' once we perceive danger. In today's modern society, this mechanism is triggered not just by the presence of real physical danger, but also by psychological danger, such as when we feel our self-esteem, long-term hopes and expectations, and how we will be viewed by others, are in danger of being frustrated or thwarted by the situation we find ourselves in. Because it is then inappropriate to actually engage in a 'fight or flight' response, we are left feeling emotionally aroused and uncomfortable until our body is given time to calm down again. As we will see later, this is why learning not to see a situation as threatening is one of the most important skills in avoiding stress. In a model of pupil stress (see Figure 6.1) I have indicated this initial appraisal process by boxes 1, 2 and 3.

The level of stress experienced by pupils will also vary from pupil to pupil. The reasons for this are that firstly, different pupils are exposed to different levels of potential stressors, and secondly, pupils will vary as to whether they view a potential stressor as a threat or not. If a pupil feels able to deal with the situation, little or no stress will be generated. For example, in the run-up to an examination, one pupil may feel very confident about passing the examination, or know that the result of the examination does not really matter because they have already secured the grades they need from the results of other examinations. In such a case, the pupil may experience little or no stress. In contrast, for another pupil, who needs a good grade in the examination but is finding the revision difficult, the level of stress may be extremely high. The personal characteristics of the pupil will also impinge on the stress process. Pupils' attitudes and needs, whether they have a personality trait that is prone to worry about things, the level of skills they have to deal with the demands they will face in school, how they were brought up, and their previous experience of dealing with potential stressors, will all impact on this appraisal process. This is illustrated in Figure 6.1 by the link between box 7 (pupil characteristics) and box 2 (appraisal).

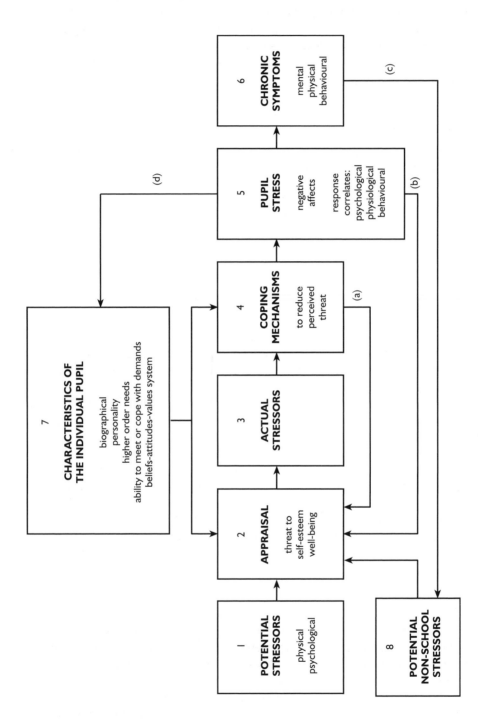

Figure 6.1 A model of pupil stress

The link between box 8 (potential non-school stressors) and box 2 (appraisal) indicates that facing potential stressors outside the school can also increase the likelihood of seeing demands in school as threatening. For example, if a pupil is experiencing problems at home such as being bullied by an older brother or having a mother who is seriously ill, such problems can have a major impact on increasing a pupil's vulnerability to stress at school.

Coping mechanisms (box 4) are the actions taken by the pupil to reduce the perceived threat, either by dealing directly with the actual stressor or indirectly by using strategies to lessen their negative feelings about the situation. The experience of pupil stress itself (box 5) is defined in terms of negative affects (emotions), such as anxiety and depression. Pupil stress also has three main correlates:

- *psychological*, e.g. lowered self-esteem
- *physiological*, e.g. increased heart rate
- *behavioural*, e.g. aggression towards others

If stress is frequent and prolonged, there is a danger that chronic symptoms of stress may develop, such as stress-related ill health (both mental and physical), as well as behavioural consequences such as disaffection, bullying and truancy (box 6).

The model also includes four important feedback loops, shown as (a), (b), (c) and (d). The first of these indicates that the coping mechanisms used by a pupil may influence their appraisal process. For example, a pupil whose method of coping is to try to deny to themselves that they face any problem in the first place may well fail to deal with new demands, and this in the longer run could lead to problems that are so serious that they are then forced to acknowledge them. Feedback loops (b), (c) and (d) indicate the way in which experiencing a high level of stress can affect pupils' appraisal process by making them feel much more sensitive and vulnerable to new demands. We all know how when we are feeling annoyed, tired or off-colour, new demands seem to be much harder to deal with and we are much more likely to regard such new demands as additional burdens which pose a threat. Indeed, a commonly cited indicator of stress is that a pupil's usual level of goodwill towards others has disappeared, and that they snap in a hostile manner at new demands which in the past they would normally have dealt with in a calm and good-humoured manner.

Stressful life events

A number of researchers have noted how stress occurring in one area of our lives can have an impact on the stress that we experience in another area. Moreover, the more separate sources of stress we have to deal with, the more likely it is that these will then generate health problems. For example, in the survey by the Office for National Statistics (Meltzer *et al.*, 2000) of mental health problems in childhood and adolescence (considered in chapter 2), data were collected on whether pupils had experienced 10 'stressful life events'. These were:

- The pupil's parent had had a separation due to marital difficulties or broken off a steady relationship.
- The pupil's parent (or partner) had had a major financial crisis such as losing the equivalent of at least three months' income.
- The pupil's parent (or partner) had had a problem with the police involving a court appearance.
- The pupil had had a serious illness which required a stay in hospital.
- The pupil had been in a serious accident or badly hurt in an accident.
- The pupil's parent, brother or sister had died.
- A close friend of the pupil had died.
- The pupil's grandparent had died.
- The pupil's pet had died.
- The pupil had broken off a steady relationship with a boyfriend or girlfriend (applied only to pupils aged 13 years or above).

For eight of these events, the proportion of pupils who had experienced the event was higher amongst those pupils who had developed a mental health disorder. For example, 50 per cent of pupils with a mental disorder had at some time seen the separation of their parents compared with 29 per cent of the sample with no disorder. Only two of the events did not reflect this trend: the death of a grandparent and the death of a pet.

However, the cumulative impact of experiencing three or more such events was crucial. The study reported that 15 per cent of the pupils had experienced three or more of these events. For this group the incidence of mental disorder was 19 per cent, compared with 7 per cent for pupils who had experienced two or fewer events. Such studies indicate how stress experienced outside school may impact on stress experienced inside school, and that the accumulation of stress from different sources increases the likelihood that the pupil will be unable to cope with the stress they experience in school and that associated health problems are more likely to occur.

Measuring pupil stress

A major problem facing researchers has been the measurement of pupil stress. Self-reported stress questionnaires have been the most widely used approach. These differ a great deal in format and content. Some have included simple and direct questions, asking the pupils to report their overall level of stress on a response scale. Others have asked pupils to report the frequency and intensity of sources of stress and/or symptoms of stress and then computed an overall measure of the level of stress from these data. In addition to self-reported questionnaires, some studies have looked at psychological, physiological and behavioural indicators of stress (such as muscular aches and pains, chronic levels of high tension and anxiety, sleeplessness and truancy).

All measures of pupil stress have their strengths and weaknesses. The widespread use of self-reported questionnaires has been very successful in generating information about pupil stress. However, given the subjectivity involved in self-report, one must be very cautious about its use in providing information about a particular pupil's level of stress. Nevertheless, the checklist in Figure 6.2 provides a useful indicator of whether a pupil is experiencing a high level of stress at school.

STRESS AT SCHOOL CHECKLIST

Rating scale
0 = Never
1 = Sometimes
2 = Often
3 = Almost every day

Rate how often you feel in the following ways using the above response scale (circle one of the numbers 0 to 3 for each item).

1.	I find myself worrying a lot about problems at school	0 1 2 3
2.	I feel work at school is affecting my home life	0 1 2 3
3.	At the end of a school day I feel emotionally exhausted	0 1 2 3
4.	The school day seems to be one hassle after another	0 1 2 3
5.	I get very upset by problems during the school day	0 1 2 3
6.	I wake up at nights thinking about problems at school	0 1 2 3
7.	I feel overloaded with the schoolwork that needs to be done	0 1 2 3
8.	I get tense and frustrated by events at school	0 1 2 3
9.	I feel my school is affecting my health	0 1 2 3
10.	I feel I am unable to cope with all the demands at school	0 1 2 3

Total score
Less than 5: low level of stress
5 to 15:   moderate level of stress
Above 15:   high level of stress

Figure 6.2 Pupil stress checklist

What are the main causes of pupil stress?

Much of the early work on pupil stress in the UK focused on two areas. The first area deals with the stress generated by tests and examinations. This has for many years been the most dominant area of research on pupil stress, and this remains the case now. The second area deals with starting school and moving to a new school.

Examination stress

Denscombe (2000) in a study of 15–16-year-old pupils in the East Midlands used questionnaire responses from 1648 Year 10 and 11 pupils together with some follow-up interviews to explore their views of the major hazards to their health. Mental stress was rated as the highest hazard by female pupils and the fourth highest hazard by male pupils. In exploring the sources of mental stress with these pupils, Denscombe reported that taking GCSEs constituted the major source of stress, with its mixture of examination and coursework pressures and the pupils' perception that their success or otherwise in their GCSEs constituted a fateful moment in their life trajectories. Similarly, a number of studies have also pointed to the high levels of stress and anxiety generated by tests and examinations taken in the primary school years (e.g. Eady, 1999).

There has been a wealth of research on 'test anxiety' over the years. McDonald (2001) argues that test anxiety has two main components. The first is a cognitive component based on how the pupil thinks that poor grades might affect their self-concept and have implications for their future life choices (e.g. 'If I do badly on this test my friends will think I am stupid' and 'Without a good grade in this exam I will not be able to go to university'). The second component is emotionality (e.g. elevated heart rate, sweating, feeling sick and shaking). Test anxiety usually acts as an important motivator for pupils to work hard. The danger is that high levels of test anxiety can lead to underperforming in tests through nervousness and can also contribute to truancy and school refusal.

Transfer stress

The second main area of early work on pupil stress has been the stress generated by starting primary school at the age of 5 years and the transfer from primary to secondary school at the age of 11 years. Much of the stress here was generated by pupils' fears about whether they would be intimidated or bullied by older pupils, whether the work would be too difficult for them to cope with, and whether the teachers would be very strict. As a result of such research, it is very common now for both primary schools and secondary schools to have in place a number of schemes, which usually include visits to the new school, so that such fears can be allayed and pupils can become more informed and familiar with the new school before they actually start there.

Gross and Burdett (1996) looked at areas of concern reported by 75 Year 6 pupils prior to and just after transfer from three primary schools to a secondary school. The main concerns before transfer were friends, work, teasing, bullying, showers, and injections/medicals. Each area of concern was markedly lower when revisited after half a term in their new school. After the transfer, the pupils were also asked how they had coped in response to the problems they had faced. The main coping strategies they reported using were seeking social support, problem solving, and cognitive restructuring.

A study of 120 Year 7 pupils at the end of their second term after transfer to a secondary school in London by Karagiannopoulou (1999) highlighted the role that the family plays in helping pupils adjust to life in a new school. Her study indicated that transfer stress was highest amongst those pupils who had an anxious personality. More interesting, however, was that pupils whose family were categorised as coherent and flexible rarely experienced high stress after transfer, whilst pupils from families categorised as unbalanced (i.e. either chaotic or rigid) were likely to continue to experience stress beyond the first term after transfer. This study reminds us of the important role played by families in helping pupils to cope with new demands and changes arising from schooling.

Academic demands and relationships

Some studies of pupil stress have tried to gain a much broader picture of the worries and concerns that are generated in schools, dealing with the academic demands made on pupils in the classroom, and the relationships that pupils are able to establish with teachers and peers both inside the classroom and in the wider setting of the school.

Gallagher and Millar (1996) surveyed the social and personal worries of 3983 pupils aged 13 to 18 years in Northern Ireland. The most frequent worries reported dealt with schoolwork and examinations, followed by worries about the future in terms of what type of job they would end up doing and the type of further and higher education courses they would be able to take. Various studies have indicated that these worries about the future increase during the secondary school years, and are acute for those pupils intending to leave school at the end of compulsory schooling, who expect to achieve low examination grades, and who live in an area of high youth unemployment (Kyriacou and Butcher, 1993). Such stress is also acute in countries where there is intense competition to gain entry to the top universities, such as Japan, where achieving good examination grades can still be seen as relative failure. Gallagher and Millar also reported that for their sample, personal worries to do with self-image were relatively infrequent, suggesting that most of the adolescents had a positive self-concept.

A study by Murberg (in preparation) looked at pupil stress amongst 535 secondary school pupils in Norway aged 13 to 16 years. The sources of stress were grouped into four areas, listed below in order of the overall levels of stress reported for each of them (starting with the highest):

- pressure to achieve good results at school
- school workload pressure
- difficulties with parents and/or teachers related to school
- difficulties with peers and/or other pupils.

Murberg reported that pupils' stress in each area was associated with the experience of psychosomatic symptoms, such as headaches and back pains.

A study by Kim (2002) of 116 secondary school pupils aged 16 to 17 years in South Korea reported that the main sources of stress were:

- the stress of working hard
- worries about the pupil's future life
- worries about further education
- the stress of studying
- problems with a specific subject.

Kim also reported that pupils' overall level of stress was associated with the experience of psychosomatic symptoms, such as headaches and back pains (using a list of symptoms of the type reported above by Murberg for pupils in Norway).

A study by Kyriacou and Moutantzi (2003) used a questionnaire and follow-up interviews with 50 primary school pupils aged 8 to 9 years in England and Greece to explore the day-to-day sources of stress generated by classroom activities. Overall, the circumstances which generated the most stress were:

- being told off by a teacher when you are naughty
- getting work back from a teacher that has lots of mistakes
- taking a test
- not knowing the answer to a teacher's question.

Pollard *et al.* (2000), in a study which included 54 primary school pupils interviewed in each of Years 3 to 6 (i.e. when aged 7 to 11 years), grouped their worries about school work into seven categories:

- appearance (e.g. work looks scruffy)
- correctness (e.g. lots of red crosses)
- quantity (e.g. when I don't do as much as Miss wants)
- quality (e.g. if the story isn't interesting)
- understanding (e.g. getting stuck)
- distraction/interference (e.g. if I've been chatting)
- fear of exposure (e.g. someone saying it's not good).

Appearance and correctness were the most frequent worries when the pupils were in Year 3, but by the time they had reached Year 6 their worries were almost exclusively about understanding.

What can schools do to help pupils who experience high levels of stress and to reduce pupil stress?

A number of studies have explored ways in which pupils attempt to cope with the stress they experience in schools and have also evaluated some interventions aimed at helping pupils to develop effective coping strategies.

Coping strategies

Coping strategies can be divided into two main categories: *direct-action* and *palliative techniques*. Direct action involves identifying the source of stress and then taking action that deals effectively with the source of the problem. For example, if a pupil is worried about not being able to keep up with the work, devoting more time to doing the work, getting advice or help from someone else with the work (including extra tuition), or explaining the problem to the teacher so that less is demanded, are all forms of direct action. In general, direct action is the best way to deal with stress because, when it is successful, it actually eliminates the problem. However, some sources of stress may not be successfully dealt with by direct action. In these circumstances, palliative techniques are helpful. Palliative techniques do not deal with the source of the stress, but rather aim to reduce the emotional experience which it generates. The most powerful palliative techniques are to put things in perspective and to have a sense of humour, so that the problem appears to be less serious or important. Engaging in activities that can help take your mind off a problem can also be helpful. In addition, some relaxation and emotion control techniques that help the body to unwind and feel less tense are useful. In these cases, the source of stress remains, but the reaction to it is reduced.

Frydenberg and Lewis (1999) explored the coping strategies of 829 secondary school pupils aged 11 to 18 years in Australia, which were identified in terms of 18 categories of coping. The order of frequency of their use was as follows:

- work hard and achieve
- focus on solving the problem
- wishful thinking
- invest in close friends
- seek to belong
- worry
- seek social support
- focus on the positive
- tension reduction
- seek relaxing diversions
- keep to self
- not cope
- self-blame
- ignore the problem
- physical recreation
- seek spiritual support
- social action
- seek professional help.

Of course, a high frequency of use does not necessarily mean that a coping strategy is more effective, nor that what is effective for one pupil will be equally effective for another. The effectiveness of a coping strategy depends on a complex interaction between the nature of the main sources of stress facing a particular pupil, the circumstances in which these occur, and aspects of the pupil's personality.

Boekaerts (1995) has made a distinction between, on the one hand, positive responses to stress which focus on problem solving and developing mastery of the situation and, on the other hand, maladaptive responses, which focus on worrying and allowing the situation to get worse. Boekaerts has called for intervention strategies to help pupils to develop positive responses. This view is supported by Parsons *et al.* (1996), who looked at the association between coping strategies and achievement for 374 pupils at a boys' independent secondary school in Melbourne, Australia. The coping strategies that correlated most positively with over-achievement (i.e. doing better than expected on the basis of IQ scores) were 'work hard and achieve', 'focus on solving the problem' and 'seek social support'. The coping strategies that correlated most negatively with over-achievement were 'not cope' and 'ignore the problem'.

Intervention strategies

A study by Leonard *et al.* (2001) focused on three intervention strategies aimed at reducing the level of stress reported by 448 primary school pupils in New South Wales, Australia. The authors argue that for many pupils the school environment can be regarded as a workplace, and interventions can help reduce their stress and stress-related absenteeism. The intervention strategies used were:

- lessons aimed at improving pupils' communication and interaction skills
- progressive relaxation, breathing and imagination exercises
- background mood music at transition periods during the school day, such as after the lunch break.

They reported that none of the three interventions had a significant effect on pupils, but the task of measuring such an effect was hampered because the pupils were generally very positive about school and had low rates of absences, so the power of these interventions to lead to a measurable change in pupils' attitudes and attendance was probably very limited.

In general, studies of schools where pupils have been helped to develop techniques for dealing with stress, both in terms of improving their direct action skills (e.g. improving their management of study time) and their palliative techniques (e.g. relaxation exercises), have yielded qualitative data from pupils which indicate that these interventions have been successful in reducing their stress, but evaluations based on quantitative measures are often equivocal and inconsistent.

For example, Kyriacou and Butcher (1993) evaluated a stress counselling course taken by 26 Year 11 pupils aged 15 to 16 years at a secondary school in the North of England, which comprised six elements:

- stress recognition
- physical fitness
- healthy diet
- effective revision
- interview preparation
- relaxation techniques, including guided imagery.

The pupils were interviewed after they had completed their GCSE examinations and reported that they found the course very useful.

Work on helping pupils to develop strategies to reduce stress has received a boost in many countries from governments which have included this as a part of the school curriculum. For example, in England, part of the framework for PSHE seeks to make the school environment a healthier place and to promote a healthier lifestyle, and explicitly includes teaching about the causes and symptoms of stress and identifying strategies for its prevention and management (DfEE, 1999a). In addition, the 'healthy schools' initiative seeks to promote better health and emotional well-being for pupils by establishing local programmes based on partnerships which link schools to a range of agencies in their local community, particularly health services (DfEE, 1999b).

A number of writers have also produced guides and manuals which outline a range of ideas and activities that can help pupils and teachers to reduce pupil stress (McNamara, 2000; Mills, 1992; Robson *et al.*, 1995; Traxson, 1999).

Mills (1992) suggests that schools undertake 'stress mapping' in which they predict stress events and situations that will occur for pupils during the school year. This can then help alert teachers to signs of pupil stress at these times, and also enable the school to explore whether organisational arrangements can be adjusted to minimise the stress that may be generated. Events such as the end-of-year examinations will clearly need to feature in stress mapping. Other events can include tests, coursework deadlines, the period just after school reports have been sent to parents, meetings with parents, option choices, news of the allocation to new classes (particularly if these involve setting or streaming) and changes of teacher. At times of stress, the school should avoid placing other demands on pupils which can be better timed for another part of the year. Thus, for example, activities such as a sports day or a school play should not be timed to take place just before coursework deadlines or examinations. However, some schools have deliberately timetabled a school outing to take place at these times, in part to act as a distractor from a stress event, although this has to be organised carefully so that it does not interfere with other coping strategies that pupils may prefer to use, such as trying to be well prepared for the demands ahead. Making use of a school council or some other group of pupil representatives can enable pupils to draw to the attention of teachers the ways in which organisational factors in the school can be creating unnecessary stress.

It is also important to note that the physical environment of the school can have an impact in reducing stress. An environment in which a pupil can feel safe and relaxed will help to minimise stress. A school with such an environment has the following characteristics:

- Pupils are able to move around the building easily in order to get to their classrooms on time.
- The physical environment looks well cared for (walls recently painted, floors carpeted, flower displays, rooms and corridors well lit).
- Break times can be taken in comfort, with play areas that are secure, well supervised, and protected from rain.

- Noise levels are low (carpeting will help here, and the sound of ringing to indicate lesson breaks should not be ear-piercing).

Similarly, the social environment of the school is important. In particular, teachers who generally seem to be friendly, who smile, are on good terms with pupils and are accessible when problems occur will do much to help pupils feel safe and relaxed.

In working with pupils to enhance their coping strategies, the teacher needs to be careful not to preach to pupils. Rather, group discussion should be used to enable pupils to explore their feelings about sources of stress, and in doing so to recognise how common such feelings are amongst their peers, which in itself can be reassuring. In addition, the teacher needs to make clear that such discussion is confidential, but if a particular pupil has a concern that they wish to disclose to a teacher in private, the teacher needs to outline the options for doing this.

ACTION POINTS

Improving the school environment

This involves helping pupils to contribute to making the school a friendly environment that promotes positive pupil–pupil and teacher–pupil interactions. This will highlight the need to be nice and supportive towards others, to avoid teasing and using put-downs. It will also include improving the physical environment, so that it is pleasant and well cared for.

Promoting a healthy life style

This includes promoting healthy eating habits, physical exercise, avoiding drugs, smoking and alcohol, and developing enjoyable interests outside school.

Developing good work habits

This involves developing habits to ensure that work is done to a good standard and in good time. This will include developing time-management skills, such as prioritising tasks, planning work and revision timetables, and avoiding procrastination.

Enhancing pupils' self-esteem

Pupils with a low self-esteem are particularly vulnerable to stress. Activities aimed at helping pupils to feel self-confident and to value themselves will provide an important buffer to stress.

Improving pupils' communication skills

Much stress arises from genuine misunderstandings and from pupils' inability to articulate their needs and concerns to others. Helping pupils to express their views and concerns clearly to other pupils and to teachers will help to prevent such misunderstandings and will also enable problems to be resolved more easily.

Targeting sources of stress

This involves both pupils and teachers together identifying sources of stress for pupils that the school can do something about. For example, ensuring that course work deadlines are staggered across subjects; that areas of the playground are properly supervised; that pupils have somewhere safe to leave their property; and that teachers' expectations are made clear.

Raising stress awareness

This involves helping pupils to identify their own sources of stress and to develop effective strategies to deal with these. All pupils will become upset from time to time, be it in the form of anger, anxiety or depression. Pupils need to be able to recognise this, to think about what might be causing them stress, and to consider what action they can take to deal with any problems they face.

Relaxation training

Training in relaxation techniques, included guided imagery, can be helpful, for example imagining a peaceful location that you can go to to relax, or developing breathing exercises.

Counselling

Some pupils may need professional support in the form of counselling in order to come to terms with their circumstances. Teachers involved in running stress-management workshops and in supporting pupils with problems need to know about referral agencies available to assess whether a pupil may need therapeutic counselling.

School policy on crisis management

This involves having a school action plan to deal with the aftermath of potentially traumatising events, such as fatal accidents. The policy and/or the action plan needs to outline the decisions that will need to be taken; create channels of communication that will keep everyone informed about what happened, is happening and its consequences; allocate key tasks to individual members of staff; ensure that contact is made with appropriate support agencies, including counsellors; and ensure that the school is kept running as normally as possible and/or its functioning is modified as appropriate.

References

Boekaerts, M. (1995) 'Affects, emotions and learning.' In L. W. Anderson (ed.) *International Encyclopaedia of Teaching and Teacher Education*, 2nd edn (pp. 402–07). Oxford: Pergamon.

Bru, E., Boyesen, M., Munthe, E. and Roland, E. (1998) 'Perceived social support at school and emotional and musculoskeletal complaints among Norwegian 8th grade students.' *Scandinavian Journal of Educational Research*, 42(2), 339–56.

Denscombe, M. (2000) 'Social conditions for stress: young people's experience of doing GCSEs.' *British Educational Research Journal*, 26(3), 359–74.

DfEE (1999a) *The National Curriculum.* London: DfEE.

DfEE (1999b) *National Healthy School Standard: Guidance.* London: DfEE.

Eady, S. (1999) 'An investigation of possible correlation of general anxiety with performance in eleven-plus scores in year 6 primary school pupils.' *Educational Psychology*, 19(3), 347–59.

Frydenberg, E. and Lewis, R. (1999) 'Things don't get better just because you're older: a case for facilitating reflection.' *British Journal of Educational Psychology*, 69(1), 81–94.

Gallagher, M. and Millar, R. (1996) 'A survey of adolescent worry in Northern Ireland.' *Pastoral Care in Education*, 14(2), 26–32.

Gross, H. and Burdett, G. (1996) 'Coping with school transfer: predicting and using coping strategies.' *Pastoral Care in Education*, 14(3), 38–44.

Hodge, G. M., McCormick, J. and Elliot, R. (1997) 'Examination-induced distress in a public examination at the completion of secondary schooling.' *British Journal of Educational Psychology*, 67(2), 185–97.

Karagiannopoulou, E. (1999) 'Stress on transfer from primary to secondary school: the contribution of A-trait, life events and family functioning.' *Psychology of Education Review*, 23(2), 27–32.

Kim, J. (2002) *Pupils' Stress and Worries at Secondary School in South Korea.* MA dissertation. York: University of York.

Kinchin, D. and Brown, E. (2001) *Supporting Children with Post-traumatic Stress Disorder: A Practical Guide for Teachers and Professionals.* London: David Fulton.

Kyriacou, C. and Butcher, B. (1993) 'Stress in year 11 school children.' *Pastoral Care in Education*, 11(3), 19–21.

Kyriacou, C. and Moutantzi, G. (2003) 'Pupil stress in the primary school classroom in England and Greece.' *Education Today*, 53(1), 44–6.

Leonard, C., Bourke, S. and Schofield, N. (2001) 'The effect of stress management and relaxation techniques on student quality of life and absenteeism in primary schools.' Paper presented at the 9th European Conference for Research on Learning and Instruction, Fribourg, Switzerland, 28 August–1 September.

McDonald, A. S. (2001) 'The prevalence and effects of text anxiety in school children.' *Educational Psychology*, 21(1), 89–101.

McNamara, S. (2000) *Stress in Young People: What's New and What Can We Do?* London: Continuum.

Meltzer, H., Gatward, R., Goodman, R. and Ford, T. (2000) *Mental Health of Children and Adolescents in Great Britain.* London: The Stationery Office.

Mills, S. H. (1992) *Helping Pupils to Cope with Stress: A Guide for Teachers.* Lancaster: Framework Press.

Murberg, T. (in preparation) 'School-related stress and psychosomatic symptoms among Norwegian female and male adolescents.'

Parsons, A., Frydenberg, E. and Poole, C. (1996) 'Overachievement and coping strategies in adolescent males.' *British Journal of Educational Psychology*, 66(1), 109–14.

Pollard, A., Triggs, P., Broadfoot, P., McNess, E. and Osborn, M. (2000) *What Pupils Say: Changing Policy and Practice in Primary Education.* London: Continuum.

Robson, M., Cook, P. and Gilliland, J. (1995) 'Helping children manage stress.' *British Educational Research Journal*, 21(2), 165–74.

Sharp, S. and Cowie, H. (1998) *Counselling and Supporting Children in Distress.* London: Sage.

Shears, J. (1995) 'Managing a tragedy in a secondary school.' In S. C. Smith and M. Pennells (eds) *Interventions with Bereaved Children* (pp. 241–54). London: Jessica Kingsley.

Traxson, D. (1999) 'De-stressing children in the classroom.' In J. Leadbetter, S. Morris, P. Timmins, G. Knight and D. Traxson (eds) *Applying Psychology in the Classroom* (pp. 36–49). London: David Fulton.

Yule, W. and Gold, A. (1993) *Wise before the Event: Coping with Crises in Schools.* London: Calouste Gulbenkian Foundation.

7 Abuse

Estimates of the incidence of child abuse have gradually increased over the last few decades following a greater willingness of victims of such abuse to disclose it, and the widespread discussion of many well-publicised cases which were subject to legal procedures and investigations into how social services and other agencies might do more to protect children from abuse. As a consequence of this, efforts have been made to establish a more coordinated multi-agency approach to identifying and dealing with cases of suspected abuse. It is now recognised that the unique role of the school in having daily contact with pupils means that it has a key part to play in identifying a cause for concern. The frequency of abuse means that schools also need to think about how they can help pupils and their families to cope with the aftermath of such abuse. In addition, there are initiatives in place for schools to play a greater role in education for child protection, both by helping pupils to become aware of how to protect themselves against abuse and by promoting better parenting.

What do we mean by 'child abuse' and how common is it?

There are three categories of abuse: physical, emotional and sexual; and, in addition, there is a related category of neglect (DfEE, 1995; Kinchin and Brown, 2001).

Physical abuse

This involves either committing actual bodily harm or failing to prevent such harm occurring. This may including beatings, pulling of hair and burning. Indicators of physical abuse include:

- frequent unexplained injuries
- fear of being touched
- bullying younger pupils
- fear of parents being contacted
- fear of being examined
- avoiding undressing in public.

Emotional abuse

This involves persistent emotional ill-treatment. This may include denigration, insults, sarcasm and isolation. Indicators of emotional abuse include:

- stuttering
- immature behaviour

- reacting badly to criticism
- drug abuse
- passivity
- avoiding taking risks.

Sexual abuse

This involves sexual acts being committed on or in the presence of the pupil, most often by a adult relative, and less often by an older sibling or an unrelated adult. This may include sexual intercourse, masturbation and taking indecent photographs. Indicators of sexual abuse include:

- precocious references to sexual acts
- hints about personal secrets
- sexual acts towards other pupils
- emotional withdrawal
- self-harm
- becoming easily upset.

Neglect

This involves a failure to offer sufficient care which thereby endangers the child's physical and mental health and development. This may include starvation, a lack of basic hygiene, and regularly witnessing domestic violence. Indicators of neglect include:

- constant hunger
- emaciation
- obsessive rhythmic actions (such as rocking or hair twisting)
- poor attendance
- being unwashed
- poor clothing.

Estimating the incidence of abuse

In 1998 there were 31,600 children on child protection registers in England, with 29 per cent in the category of physical abuse, 15 per cent emotional, 19 per cent sexual and 37 per cent neglect. However, whilst a distinction is made between these four categories, it is important to note that they overlap in many ways, and in many cases we can refer to syndromes of abuse, since pupils experiencing one of these categories of abuse are more than likely to be also experiencing one or more of the other categories.

A study by Branwhite (1994) asked 836 Year 7 pupils aged 11 to 12 years to consider a list of 14 incidents representing potential sources of social stress and to indicate for each one whether they had experienced it and thought a lot about it afterwards. Six per cent of the pupils responded 'yes' to the incident 'having an adult do something very bad to you'.

However, estimates of the proportion of pupils who have suffered abuse or neglect (i.e. 'significant harm') during the school years are extremely difficult to make (Bonner *et al.*, 2001; Cleaver *et al.*, 1998; Wattam, 1999). If a survey asks individuals to report whether any single incident occurred which they feel constitutes abuse, and includes examples such as being smacked excessively by a parent, being belittled by a parent, seeing someone indecently exposing themselves in a public place, or being left at home alone when they were in need of care, the vast majority of adolescents will report that at least one incident has occurred. If the survey, however, is restricted to persistent abuse that they feel has significantly harmed their mental or physical health, our best estimate of the proportion seems to be about 10 per cent.

Perpetrators of abuse

Studies have sought to indicate the characteristics of abusers. Perpetrators are extremely mixed, and there is a real danger in focusing on a narrow set of typologies. Indeed, one of the reasons why much child abuse is not identified is simply a failure to recognise that apparently pleasant, sociable and loving individuals can be abusing children. The only consistent finding about abusers is that a high proportion of them have suffered from mental illness, are living in multi-disadvantaged circumstances and have experienced child abuse themselves (Cleaver *et al.*, 1998; Wattam, 1999).

Physical abuse

In identifying physical abuse, it is important to note that a concern can be raised about an injury in the first instance even when you do not have clear information about the circumstances in which the injury occurred. For example, if a pupil has a black eye and says they fell over in the playground, you can ask if anyone saw this happen and see if the story can be corroborated. In addition, if the pupil says they fell over at home, you can ask how this happened. If the pupil seems to be very reluctant to talk about such matters, or gives an explanation that sounds dubious or inconsistent, this is likely to raise concerns. It is also a cause for concern if something similar has happened before.

Neglect

The line between physical abuse and neglect is a grey one, since in cases of neglect the ill health, harm and injury which occurs may not result from the direct behaviour of the parents, but indirectly through their lack of adequate care and supervision. At its lower end, neglect will merge into what can be referred to as simply 'poor parenting'.

Emotional abuse

Distinguishing between what is emotional abuse and what is the acceptable limit of parenting is particularly problematic, and needs to take appropriate account of a range of factors impacting on the family circumstances, such as poverty, culture, and lifestyle choices. In the case of physical abuse, the identification of actual injury or harm does, at least, provide some visible evidence for concern. In the case of emotional abuse, however, the indicators are much harder to determine. In some countries, legislators have tried to define 'emotional injury' or 'emotional damage' in terms of phrases such as 'the substantial and observable impairment of the child's mental or emotional functioning', and to link this with specific actions or behaviour by parents or others such as 'inappropriate humiliation', 'exposure to severe domestic disharmony' and 'deprivation of cognitive stimulation' (Barker, 1993). However, such attempts simply serve to highlight the problems involved in producing reliable indicators of emotional abuse.

A study by Piekarska (2000) of 271 primary school pupils aged 13 to 14 years in Poland sought to explore psychological abusive behaviours by teachers and how pupils attempted to cope with these. Teachers' abusive behaviours included threats (e.g. to contact parents), mockery (e.g. being made to read out poor work in front of the class), humiliation (e.g. comments about low intelligence), insults (e.g. calling the pupil an idiot) and personal attacks (e.g. criticism of the pupil's appearance). This study serves to highlight that there is a thin line between some teachers' use of put-downs and what may constitute emotional abuse.

Sexual abuse

Sexual abuse is often difficult to identify because of the complex nature of the circumstances. The pupil may often be very confused about whether they have in some way consented to the activity and may also have reasons for wishing to conceal the abuse. They are often in a situation where the abuser has power over them and has intimidated them into accepting the abuse and keeping it a secret. The pupil may also be aware of the harm that identifying the abuser may have on the family if the abuser is a parent, relative or close family friend. They may even have been led to believe that the abuse has been condoned by other members of the family. In the case of pupils in the primary school years, they may also be quite confused about what is normal and acceptable behaviour, and lack the vocabulary to be able to explain easily to others what exactly happened to them.

A questionnaire survey of female undergraduates at Cardiff University by Oaksford and Frude (2001) found that 13 per cent of the 213 respondents reported that they had been sexually abused in childhood. A study of female undergraduates at a university in New England, USA, reported by Gibson and Leitenberg (2000), puts the figure at about 11 per cent of the 825 respondents. Such studies attempting to estimate the prevalence of sexual abuse, however, are hampered by the fact that it is hard to obtain an unbiased representative sample of respondents and to decide whether a single minor incident should count equally alongside serious persistent abuse.

In cases of sexual abuse, the abuser is male in about 95 per cent of the cases, and the victim is female in about 70 per cent of the cases. Most girls are abused by family members, whilst most boys are not, although in almost all cases the abuser is well known to the victim. What may be surprising is that in about a quarter of the cases the abuser is of a similar age to the victim, and this has important implications for schools.

Another complication is that concerns may also arise in the absence of abuse, such as when it is known that another child in the family has been abused, or when a known abuser moves into a new family. In both such cases, these children are likely to be considered to be 'at risk' and teachers will need to be alert to this.

Abuse by staff

Schools also need to be alert to the possibility of abuse by staff. Some abusers are drawn to positions of trust in which they are able to work with children, whether as teachers, youth workers or the clergy. It is essential that pupils' allegations against teachers are treated with care and investigated, whilst bearing in mind that there are cases of malicious allegations being made by pupils and parents against teachers for ulterior motives. In all cases, information needs to be carefully collected at the outset as to what may have occurred and when, and whether this can be corroborated. In the case of allegations against teachers, the appropriate guidelines will need to be followed (DfEE, 1995). Moreover, individuals guilty of behaviour that makes them a risk to pupils' safety or welfare or presents an unacceptable example to pupils can be barred by the Secretary of State from the teaching profession. This decision can be made on the basis of criminal convictions for offences such as gross indecency, and on the basis of reports from the police, employers and teacher training institutions (DfES, 2001a).

A study by Skinner (2001) investigated 16 cases of sexual abuse by a teacher which had led to the prosecution of the teacher concerned. The study highlights why victims often found it difficult to disclose the abuse and the reasons why suspicions expressed by pupils, parents and other teachers often fail to be reported or acted upon. Such reasons include the power of the alleged perpetrator, a fear that one could be over-reacting, a misplaced sense of loyalty to the teacher under suspicion, and an assumption that someone else who is better placed and more likely to be believed will eventually report these suspicions.

Consequences of persistent abuse

Four common consequences of persistent abuse are severe psychological damage, serious physical injury, self-harm (including attempted suicide) and running away from home. Indeed, these are the four key signals that alert teachers and social services to possible cases of persistent abuse. Unfortunately, some cases of persistent abuse are not identified in time to prevent the death of a child, and well-publicised investigations into such cases indicate that there are likely to be a vast number of cases of persistent abuse that never come to light.

It was noted in chapter 2 that in considering how pupils react to adverse circumstances they are facing we need to consider the pupil's *mental representation of the social world*. This is particularly true in the case of sexual abuse. Research has indicated that prolonged sexual abuse has a major impact on the development of a child's self-identity. In general, most pupils have a strong positive bias in their self-identity, in which attributes that they regard as positive (e.g. I'm clever, I'm a nice person, I'm good at sports) are also regarded as being most important to them, whereas negative attributes (e.g. I'm hopeless at French, I can't sing well, I'm fat) are regarded as least important to them. This positive bias is well illustrated in a number of studies by Fischer (2002), in which pupils are asked to describe both their positive and their negative attributes and to locate these on a grid in terms of their importance to them. Typically, pupils will place in the area labelled 'most important' a very high proportion of attributes that are positive, whilst in the area labelled 'least important' they will place attributes that are mostly negative. The neutral area in between these two typically includes a mixture of both positive and negative attributes. However, when pupils who have been sexually abused are asked to do this exercise they often display a reversal of this positive bias, by including in the 'most important' area many negative attributes and in the 'least important' area many positive attributes. Fischer has suggested that this may well reflect a coping strategy in which pupils who have been sexually abused over a long period gradually develop a belief that their negative features are important and their positive features are unimportant, and that this type of self-identity is more consistent and congruent with how they make sense of the sexual abuse they are suffering. Fischer also notes that this reversal does not seem to occur in cases of physical abuse, which he suggests may be because the more intimate and penetrative nature of sexual abuse strikes at the very core of someone's being and sense of identity. Teachers therefore need to be sensitive to the real possibility that pupils who have experienced sexual abuse may have a very negative self-image and are likely to interpret the behaviour of others towards them as negative and hostile in its intent.

Skinner (2000) conducted a study which included interviews with seven women who had been victims of child sexual abuse. Most of the victims had also suffered physical and emotional abuse. They felt the abuse had badly damaged their self-image and had led to underachievement at school. Some felt that their school could have done more to support them during the period after the disclosure and to accommodate particular needs relating to their schooling that arose in consequence.

What are the school procedures for child protection?

The Children Act 1989 places duties on a number of agencies, which include schools, to work together to investigate child abuse and to meet the needs of pupils at risk of abuse (David, 1994). The DfEE (1995) specified that in every school there should be a designated member of staff who is responsible for coordinating action within the school and liaising with other agencies, including the Area Child Protection Committee (ACPC). Although schools must have procedures for handling suspected cases of abuse of pupils, the actual responsibility for investigating such cases lies with other agencies. The DfES (2001b) guidelines on dealing with suspected cases of child abuse are as follows:

- In all cases where abuse is suspected or a sustainable allegation is made, teachers and other members of staff should report the information to the designated teacher.

- The designated teacher should refer these cases to, or discuss them with, the investigating agencies according to the procedures established by the ACPC and by the LEA.

- If the designated teacher is unsure about whether a case should be formally referred or has a general concern about a child's health or development, they can seek advice and support from the local social services department, the NSPCC or the LEA's child protection coordinator. The Education Welfare Officer may also be able to offer advice.

- Whether or not to make a referral which could activate a child protection investigation is a serious decision and will require careful judgement. Where the designated teacher is not the headteacher, they should agree the way in which the designated teacher will keep the headteacher informed of a case.

- When referring a case of suspected or alleged abuse, the designated teacher should ask to be informed of the timing of the strategy discussion between the statutory agencies which will decide whether and how to investigate. The designated teacher may wish to clarify with the investigating agencies when, how and by whom the parents and the child will be told that a referral has been made.

- A member of staff, either the designated teacher or the member of staff who knows the child best, should be prepared to contribute to the strategy discussion the school's knowledge of the child.

The teacher's role

Because teachers have day-to-day contact with pupils they are in a key position to notice signs of abuse. Adams (1995) has indicated four key aspects to the teacher's role:

- *Listening*. Teachers need to be approachable and non-judgemental in order to facilitate helpful listening, and to be aware that pupils, particularly younger ones, may find it hard to understand and express what is happening to them at home.

- *Identification*. Teachers need to be observant, and in particular to be alert to signs of distress and changes in behaviour that might indicate a cause for concern.

- *Referral*. The teacher needs to be informed about the school's procedures for child protection and refer these concerns to the child protection liaison teacher.

- *Support*. Teachers need to offer support to pupils who have been subject to abuse and help them to cope with the demands being made upon them in the school.

Because of the serious nature of abuse it is essential that careful records are kept; these need to cover what was reported, what action was taken, and what happened in response to those actions. In some cases, the teacher may be required to act as a witness if the alleged abuser is prosecuted. In a case where a teacher has directly observed an incident or had an incident reported to them, this needs to be recorded immediately. The school is obliged to indicate to parents what type of records may be kept, although what they say to parents needs to be consistent with ensuring the safety of the pupil.

The issue of confidentiality is a very important one in cases of suspected abuse. A teacher cannot offer a pupil blanket confidentiality for whatever they say. Indeed, in cases of suspected abuse the teacher has a legal obligation to share the concern with others, as appropriate.

The impact on teachers

It is important to note that the teacher designated to deal with a case can play a key role in supporting the pupil through the process, and in presenting information to other agencies. This can be very stressful for the teacher involved, and that teacher will require support to undertake such a role.

A study by Skinner (1999) involved interviews with 14 teachers who had dealt with victims of sexual abuse. Only two of these teachers were designated teachers for dealing with child protection. A problem for many of the teachers was when and how to act on information given or suspicions encountered, and the study indicated that there were a number of stages before the teacher made an official notification of concern to the designated teacher. Being involved in such cases often generated a high level of stress, which included anxiety, feeling isolated and an inability to sleep.

Identifying signs of abuse

A study by Kenny (2001) of 197 teachers in Florida, USA, presented teachers with two scenarios of legally reportable child abuse, both involving an adult touching the child's genitals, and found that many of the teachers said they would not have reported these cases. This study highlights the need for teachers to be more aware of the signs that are sufficient to warrant raising a concern.

Involving outside agencies

Once suspicions have been raised, other agencies need to be involved. Schools need to be aware that investigating suspected cases requires the coordinated action of a range of outside agencies. An urgent medical examination may need to be arranged. In addition, a social worker and a police officer may need to interview the pupil jointly. It is important that the pupils and adults concerned are interviewed in a proper manner, and that interviews with pupils are kept to a minimum. Information given to parents in the early stages of an investigation needs to be handled with care and taken in cooperation with other agencies. A multi-agency meeting will decide whether the child is at risk of abuse and whether their name will be placed on the child protection register. In cases of at-risk pupils, a child protection plan will need to be drawn up, which will involve the school.

What can schools do to help victims of child abuse and reduce child abuse?

A study by Webb and Vulliamy (2001) noted that school policies on child protection typically included the following:

- the location of a handbook of guidance
- definitions of abuse with material on signs and symptoms
- procedures for teachers to follow if abuse was suspected or disclosed, including allegations against staff
- specification of the need for accurate records and their location, and arrangements if a child on the register transferred to another school
- emphasis on the need to strive to retain a positive working relationship with the families involved.

Webb and Vulliamy also suggest that cooperation between schools and agencies can be promoted through:

- schools building up a compendium of what local agencies can offer
- joint training which explores each other's roles
- inviting an agency member to address staff about their work
- participation of the designated teacher in a multi-agency community action group
- involving a home–school support worker in inter-agency liaison work.

The school also needs to provide a supportive and caring ethos, which will make it much easier for an abused pupil to disclose abuse to a teacher at the school. Teachers need to be alert to pupils who seem to want to talk to them about a problem they have and to make sure there are times when they can be approached in this way. Wattam (1999) points out that if abused children feel a greater sense of attachment to their school they will be more likely to disclose. In addition, the presence of social workers or child welfare workers in a school can increase the accessibility of pupils to a trusted adult.

Staff training needs

School policies are crucially dependent on teachers being adequately trained to put the policies into practice. These include being aware of the signs of child abuse and being confident enough to take appropriate action when a cause for concern has arisen.

Baginsky (2000) reported that training about child protection at the level of initial teacher training appears to be widespread but very superficial; at the level of in-service training, the vast majority of designated teachers have received training, but only a minority of classroom teachers have done so.

Braun and Schonveld (1994) argue that if training is to be used to overcome the blocks which prevent teachers from making referrals, it must address the specific concerns of teachers and not simply inform them about definitions and procedures. They argue that staff need opportunities to:

- *Explore their own feelings, attitudes and values concerning abuse.* This needs to be done with sensitivity as some teachers are likely to be victims of abuse themselves. In addition, teachers need to be able to make a distinction between their own ideas concerning abuse and professional obligations.
- *Consider how best to handle a child abuse case.* This includes the practicalities, such as where the teacher can take the pupil for quiet talk and which other staff need to be kept informed.
- *Develop relationships with outside agencies.* All teachers need to have knowledge of the role of outside agencies such as the police and social services.
- *Examine LEA procedures.* Teachers need to work out how to operate the procedures by using case studies involving different levels of risk and abuse.
- *Empathise with the feelings of a pupil who is attempting to disclose abuse.* The skills involved need to cover the period prior to a referral and the period when the pupil returns to school after a referral has been made.
- *Develop skills involved in dealing with the parents after referral has been made.* This needs to include consideration of how parents are to be informed about the school's procedures for child protection.
- *Become familiar with outside agencies and resources that can offer support to the pupil, parents and staff.* This will enable referrals for such support to be made.
- *Examine how child protection issues should be included in the curriculum.* The issues raised by the training will enable teachers to consider more effectively the role of education for child protection.
- *Evaluate the school's child protection policy in the light of issues raised by the training.* An evaluation of the school's procedure will both improve the procedures and enable the key issues raised by the training to be consolidated.

Braun and Schonveld note that it is common for such training to be organised and delivered by the designated teacher, but this can sometimes be problematic because it is often hard to act as a facilitator with colleagues on such sensitive issues. It can therefore be very helpful if the training is delivered by an outsider. However, outsiders will need to be carefully briefed about the school's perspective and circumstances and the training needs of the staff.

It is also important for staff training to alert teachers to cultural differences which may make disclosure more difficult for pupils from particular ethnic minorities, such as those where there is a strong tradition of respect for and obedience to adults. For example, a study by Tang (2002) explored the prevalence of child sexual abuse reported by 2147 college students in Hong Kong. Tang noted that about 6 per cent of her sample reported such abuse, with the majority of incidents occurring during the teenage years. Of these victims, only 39 per cent reported the abuse to others, and 56 per cent of the reported incidents were not followed up. Tang makes the point that in Chinese society, traditional cultural traditions and moral principles such as obedience to their parents, the suppression of sexuality, and pressure within the family to protect the family from shame may be conducive to child sexual abuse, and at the same time may lead to a much stronger reluctance on the part of victims to disclose such abuse, particularly in talking about such intimate matters to someone outside the family, such as a teacher. Consequently, amongst certain ethnic minority groups in the UK, social workers drawn from the same ethnic background as the victim of abuse may have a crucial role to play in following up any causes for concern identified by the school.

Education for pupils in protection strategies

Adams (1995) has identified eleven aspects of the PSHE curriculum which can help pupils to be less vulnerable to abuse in a range of contexts:

- the family
- relationships
- gender issues
- personal identity and self-esteem
- human/children's rights
- my body
- safety
- assertiveness
- parenthood/child-rearing
- secrets
- feelings.

Hatwin and Wyse (1998) highlight the development of self-protection strategies which include looking at dangerous situations, the difference between 'stranger danger' and 'non-stranger danger', notions of comfort and discomfort, and what pupils can do in such situations to protect themselves.

Teaching about such matters, however, is very problematic and there are differences of opinion amongst teachers, parents and other agencies concerning the type of information and material that should be drawn to the attention of pupils at different ages (Johnson, 2000). There is a real danger that certain information or material may in itself arouse worries and anxieties in pupils, and may make them more sensitive to misinterpreting the normal behaviour of others around them as abusive. The point has also been made that some educational campaigns may be misleading. For example, the idea of 'stranger danger' may mislead some young pupils into thinking that certain types of adults who approach them in the street constitute the main or only source of danger to them, when in fact most sexual abusers are well known to the victim and are relatives or friends of the family.

In addition, some parents may have strong views concerning whether teaching about such issues in school is appropriate, and, if so, what ideas should be covered and how. Those schools which decide to offer such education will therefore need to ensure that the teaching is handled with extreme care, and parents and staff will need to be involved in consenting to what is offered.

Procedures to deal with suspected abuse

All schools need to have a policy on the procedures to be followed in dealing with suspected cases of child abuse.

Support for an abused pupil

A pupil who is suspected of being abused or who has been abused will require a high level of support and careful monitoring, so that the school does not place additional demands on the pupil that will be difficult to cope with. Abused children will need to feel safe and secure at school. The pupil may be facing additional distress if they are being placed in care and if a prosecution for child abuse is taking place. Despite being the victim, the pupil may blame themselves and may be blamed by others for the situation that has occurred. There is also a high risk that an abused child in the later years of secondary schooling may be considering running away from home. Depending on the degree of trauma involved and the length of the abuse, therapeutic counselling may also be required. The school will need to liaise with the parents or carers, as appropriate, and with the other agencies involved.

After-school supervision

After-school provision can play a useful part in providing a safe and secure environment for young pupils during a few hours at the end of the school day, which can be of immense value to pupils who are unable to gain entry to their own homes until much later in the day. Such provision can also enable some pupils to spend less time in a home situation where they may be subject to abuse. The informal nature of some types of after-school supervision can often also make it easier for the pupil to disclose the abuse they are experiencing to a teacher or other adult supervisor. Some intervention programmes based on after-school supervision can also provide some limited access to food and drink which, in a small way, can offset some of the neglect they may be experiencing at home.

Staff training

Designated teachers and headteachers need to be trained about their role in dealing with suspected cases of abuse, and be familiar with the role of the other agencies involved. In addition, all staff in a school (teachers, governors, lunchtime supervisors) need to receive basic awareness training about the signs of abuse and the school's procedures for dealing with suspected abuse.

Education through the curriculum

Many programmes have been developed aimed at helping pupils to recognise what is happening to them if they are abused and to act appropriately to avoid danger. Nevertheless, teaching about such matters is controversial, and schools offering such education need to do so with great sensitivity and with the consent of the teachers and parents. It is possible, however, to introduce some elements of child abuse education by dealing with positive areas of the PSHE curriculum, such as family relationships, bodily changes and sex education, where issues can be covered in a way which will indirectly raise pupils' awareness of abuse, and how to be assertive and to disclose, without needing to make this explicit.

Supporting good parenting skills

Many parents can benefit from advice and guidance on how to deal with their children at home without resorting to physical and emotional abuse. Some schools make use of PSHE packs which pupils can use to undertake activities with their parents at home that can help promote good parent–child relationships and in particular help both parents and their children to develop effective conflict-resolution strategies. In addition, schools can act as a useful channel to provide parents with information packs about how they can support their children's personal development. This can also be linked to the work of other agencies in the community, and associated workshops or one-to-one sources of advice can be targeted at particular parents whose children appear to be at risk of abuse.

Monitoring adults who have contacts with pupils

All adults working as teachers are vetted to check that they are not barred from working as a teacher. In addition, however, teachers need to be vigilant about any adult who is in contact with pupils, whether on school premises or on school visits and outings. Any signs that raise concerns need to be acted upon appropriately.

References

Adams, S. (1995) 'Child protection.' In R. Best, P. Lang, C. Lodge and C. Watkins (eds) *Pastoral Care and Personal-Social Education: Entitlement and Provision* (pp. 171–89). London: Cassell.

Baginsky, M. (2000) 'Training teachers in child protection.' *Child Abuse Review*, 9(1), 74–81.

Barker, P. (1993) 'The effects of child abuse.' In V. Varma (ed.) *How and Why Children Fail* (pp. 90–102). London: Jessica Kingsley.

Bonner, B. L., Logue, M. B., Kaufman, K. L. and Niec, L. N. (2001) 'Child maltreatment.' In C. E. Walker and M. C. Roberts (eds) *Handbook of Clinical Child Psychology*, 3rd edn (pp. 989–1030). Chichester: Wiley.

Branwhite, T. (1994) 'Bullying and student distress: beneath the tip of the iceberg.' *Educational Psychology*, 14(1), 59–71.

Braun, D. and Schonveld, A. (1994). 'Training teachers in child protection: INSET.' In T. David (ed.) *Protecting Children from Abuse: Multi-Professionalism and the Children Act 1989* (pp. 91–5). Stoke-on-Trent: Trentham.

Cleaver, H., Wattam, C., Cawson, P. and Gordon, R. (1998) *Assessing Risk in Child Protection.* London: NSPCC.

David, T. (ed.) (1994) *Protecting Children from Abuse: Multi-Professionalism and the Children Act 1989.* Stoke-on-Trent: Trentham.

DfEE (1995) *Protecting Children from Abuse: The Role of the Education Service. DfEE Circular 10/95.* London: DfEE.

DfES (2001a) *Preventing Unsuitable People from Working with Children and Young Persons: Guidance for Education Staff.* London: DfES.

DfES (2001b) *Child Protection.* DfES website: www.dfes.gov.uk/a-z/atozindex.html.

Fischer, K. (2002) 'Learning and self-organization as motivations that shape development.' Paper presented at the conference 'Development and Motivation: Joint Perspectives' organised by the University of Lancaster, Department of Educational Research, held at Bowness-on-Windermere, Cumbria, 16–18 April.

Gibson, L. E. and Leitenberg, H. (2000) 'Child sexual abuse prevention programs: do they decrease the occurrence of child sexual abuse?' *Child Abuse and Neglect*, 24(9), 1115–25.

Hatwin, A. and Wyse, D. (1998) 'Child protection: the teacher's role.' *Education 3–13*, 26(3), 15–22.

Johnson, B. (2000) 'Using video vignettes to evaluate children's personal safety knowledge: methodological and ethical issues.' *Child Abuse and Neglect*, 24(6), 811–27.

Kenny, M. C. (2001) 'Child abuse reporting: teachers' perceived deterrents.' *Child Abuse and Neglect*, 25(1), 81–92.

Kinchin, D. and Brown, E. (2001) *Supporting Children with Post-traumatic Stress Disorder: A Practical Guide for Teachers and Professionals.* London: David Fulton.

Oaksford, K. L. and Frude, N. (2001) 'The prevalence and nature of child sexual abuse: evidence from a female university sample in the UK.' *Child Abuse Review*, 10(1), 49–59.

Piekarska, A. (2000) 'School stress, teachers' abusive behaviours, and children's coping strategies.' *Child Abuse and Neglect*, 24(11), 1443–9.

Skinner, J. M. (1999) 'Teachers coping with sexual abuse issues.' *Educational Research*, 41(3), 329–39.

Skinner, J. M. (2000) *Coping with Survivors and Surviving.* London: Jessica Kingsley.

Skinner, J. M. (2001) 'Teachers who abuse: impact on school communities.' *Educational Research*, 43(2), 161–74.

Tang, C. S. (2002) 'Childhood experience of sexual abuse among Hong Kong Chinese college students.' *Child Abuse and Neglect*, 26(1), 23–37.

Wattam, C. (1999) 'The prevention of child abuse.' *Children and Society*, 13(4), 317–29.

Webb, R. and Vulliamy, G. (2001) 'The primary teacher's role in child protection.' *British Educational Research Journal*, 27(1), 59–77.

8 Bereavement

The death of a loved one is one of the most painful experiences that we can encounter. Most people who experience a bereavement will get over this in time and come to terms with the loss. However, for some people the sense of grief can have a marked long-term effect on their behaviour. They may become bitter and aggressive towards others, or they may be withdrawn and reclusive, and the hurt and pain generated by the bereavement may last for many years. It has long been recognised that the effect of a bereavement on a child can be just as powerful and as long lasting as it is for an adult, and a number of initiatives have been developed to enable schools to support better those pupils who experience such a loss. There is little doubt that people nowadays are ill prepared for the death of a loved one. Western society has often been described as having a death-denying culture in which we rarely talk about the inevitability of death or about individuals who have died (Leaman,1995). Those who are bereaved often find it hard to talk to others about it, and others equally find it hard to talk to them. Indeed, some have described death as the last great taboo subject, and talking about it is still widely considered to be in bad taste. This often makes it hard for adults both to come to terms with their own response to the loss and to support their children's response to the loss.

How do children react to a bereavement?

Pupils' reactions to the loss of a loved one depend very much on the age of the pupil, their personality, the nature of the relationship they had with the loved one, and the role that other family members can play in supporting the pupil to deal with this loss. In addition, there may be powerful defence mechanisms triggered by the experience which help them to cope, and these may mask their true feelings. Consequently we need to be cautious about the notion of a typical reaction by a child to a bereavement.

The loss of a parent

Children often find it difficult to cope with the death of a parent because they find it hard to make sense of what has happened and are much more uncertain about the consequences for them and their sense that they live in a safe world where their parents will be there to love and look after them. At a young age, children have clearly had less chance to come across the idea of death or to have had experience of the death of a close relative. Even when the death has followed a period of illness, the child may have been sheltered from knowledge about the likelihood of death occurring, and as such be unprepared. Whilst the death of a parent is often a great shock, the natural resilience of a child can sometimes protect them from the intense feeling of loss that an adult experiences.

A study by Holland (2001) used questionnaires and interviews to explore the experiences of 70 adults who had experienced a parental bereavement whilst at school. Holland identified five types of loss:

- loss based on attachment and separation
- loss based on the cognitive and experiential stage of the child
- collateral or secondary losses
- losses only appreciated later in life
- losses relating to the loss of future expectations.

A key feature of Holland's study was the degree of powerlessness that the subjects reported, together with not really understanding what was happening at the time of the death. However, it is important to note that as the adults in this study had all volunteered to take part, it may be that the level of unresolved grief in such a sample may account for this.

The loss of a brother or sister

The death of a brother or sister can sometimes be even more traumatising than the death of a parent, particularly if the sibling is of the same sex and close in age. Children can often have an extremely close relationship with a brother or sister, and the change to their daily routines and sense of companionship serves as a continual reminder of the loss which has occurred. In contrast, the relationship with a parent, particularly the father, can sometimes be more distant, and as long as the surviving parent is able to cope well, the immediate disruption can be minimised more easily.

The loss of a grandparent

The death of a grandparent can also be a significant bereavement in some cases. Again this will depend on the role that the grandparent played in the family. A study by Renzenbrink (2002) looked at the responses of 21 pupils aged 8 to 13 years to the death of a grandparent. Renzenbrink's findings indicate that pupils often wanted more information about the circumstances of the death and felt that their parents were not telling them everything. The pupils were also protective of their parents, made an effort to be well behaved, and avoided asking their parents questions they thought might upset them. Particularly interesting are the accounts by pupils of how much they missed their grandparents, and that some of the pupils felt that it was harder for them to 'get over' the death than it was for their parents. In addition, some of the pupils were upset at being excluded from the funerals. Renzenbrink argues that schools need to do more to recognise how close the relationship is between some pupils and their grandparents and to be aware of the need to support pupils when such a death occurs.

Pupils' responses to a death

The type of response will vary greatly from child to child. The child's reaction will be affected by their age, whether the death was sudden, and the type of relationship they had with both the dead person and the surviving relatives. A typical response will initially involve a mixture of shock, anger and disbelief, gradually followed by feelings of grief, sorrow, loss and despair. An extract from one school's guidance for staff on dealing with a bereavement is given in Figure 8.1. The strength and length of the mourning process will depend on a variety of factors, such as whether images of the precise circumstances of the death and feelings of guilt begin to intrude.

An unexpected death has a particular high risk of impacting badly on pupils because it can shake their sense of predictability in their life, and may undermine their sense of trust in the world around them. It may also take much longer to overcome the sense of disbelief, and pupils may have dreams from which they can wake up quite confused about whether someone who has died is in fact still alive after all.

The process of mourning

Holland (1997) notes that there appear to be four central tasks to the process of mourning:

- to accept the reality of loss
- to experience the pain of grief
- to adjust to a new environment
- to invest in new relationships.

Holland warns that a pupil's reaction to a death can be confused if adults do not explain what has happened in language that the pupil can understand (e.g. how can a heart be attacked?) and if they use euphemisms for death which a child cannot interpret correctly (e.g. he's gone to sleep).

Gradually, a child will begin to adjust to the loss. However, it is likely that some degree of general insecurity about the world around them may persist, and they may react with anxiety if they think they might be separated from someone they love. If the feelings of anger or guilt persist they can be turned inwards, and there is a danger of the child becoming withdrawn, detached and depressed, or they can be turned outwards, into hostile, aggressive and anti-social behaviour towards others. If either response is extreme and prolonged, professional support will be required.

Wagner (1995) points out that when a significant bereavement occurs in the family the pupil is at risk in two ways. Firstly, because of the effects of bereavement on their concentration, feelings and behaviour. Secondly, because of their dependence on the adults who look after them to understand and meet their needs.

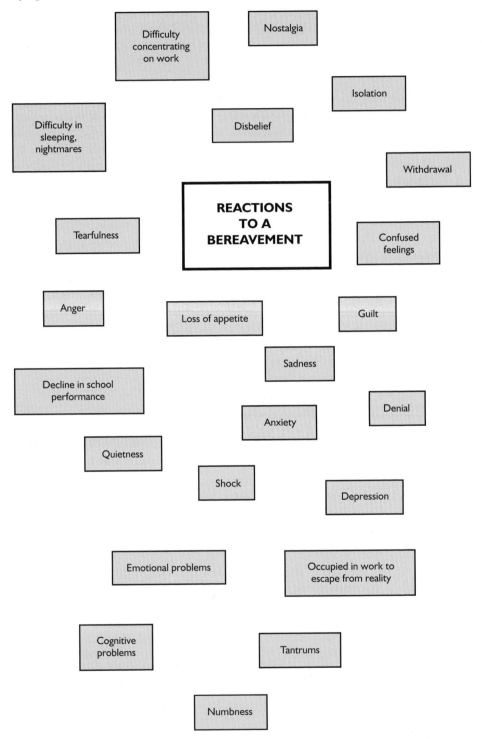

Figure 8.1   Reactions to a bereavement

The family context

In significant bereavements, parents and other siblings will also be involved in the bereavement, and the child will sometimes feel called upon to offer support and comfort to their grieving relatives rather than to work through their own grief. The child's role in the family may also need to change. For example, an older sibling may have to take more responsibility for looking after their younger brother or sister, and helping out with various domestic tasks.

When a parent has died, the pupil is likely to feel very vulnerable, and become anxious about the surviving parent dying. In these circumstances a young child might find it very difficult to tolerate being separated from the surviving parent, and may become clinging and reluctant to go to school. Older children may also start to worry about their own mortality. If the surviving parent becomes ill, this can immediately generate a high level of anxiety.

Stages of mourning

A number of studies have sought to explore the nature of bereavement and whether there are typical stages that a child will go through. Mallon (1998) identifies three main stages of mourning:

- *early grief:* the protest phase
- *acute grief:* the disorganisation phase
- *subsiding grief:* the reorganisation phase.

However, she warns that these stages are not rigid, and a teacher should not expect a pupil to progress through them in a easily recognisable fashion. A pupil may appear to be at one stage one day and revert to another the next. Nevertheless, they do act as a guide to the reactions a teacher might encounter. Mallon has outlined ways in which parents and others can work on dreams which are causing distress to help pupils through the process of mourning.

In general, however, most studies of bereavement in childhood indicate that it is a complex process with no clearly identifiable stages through which a pupil progresses in a fixed and rigid order, and that the age of the pupil and the context of the death both have a large impact on the nature of the experience (Brown, 1999; Gudas and Koocher, 2001).

The resilience of children

There is still a widespread assumption that children, in comparison with adults, are in some ways protected from the need to grieve because being young they do not fully understand what is happening and they also have the resilience of youth to move on with their lives. In contrast, the impact on adults is assumed to be much deeper because they would have had a greater emotional attachment to the person who has died. These assumptions can sometimes lead to the need for children to grieve being overlooked, and children can be expected at an early stage to simply carry on as normal and make whatever adjustments are needed. In some cases these assumptions are to some extent valid. However, in many cases they are not, and there are many instances of unresolved grief which can continue well into adulthood that stem from children not being able to mourn their loss properly at the time.

Factors that can interfere with mourning

Kinchin and Brown (2001) have listed a number of factors that can interfere with or complicate a child's mourning:

- diminished coping capacities as a result of shock
- heightened sense of vulnerability and loss of security
- realisation that the world is unpredictable
- the senseless of the event
- having unfinished business such as wishing they had said goodbye properly
- trying to reconstruct the sequence of events to understand what happened
- determining who was to blame for the death
- secondary losses such as loss of home or financial worries.

Multiple deaths

Needless to say, a multiple death, such as following a car accident when both parents have died, can be horrific and traumatising. A multiple death can lead to what some have described as 'bereavement overload'. An additional complication here is the notion of 'survivor guilt', which involves trying to come to terms with, understand and accept why they have survived when other members of their family have died. In such circumstances, survivors feel there is some hidden purpose to their surviving, that there is a sense of intentionality involved, and sometimes that they are being punished by a force they do not understand.

Estimating the incidence of bereavements

Approximately 3 per cent of pupils will suffer a significant bereavement, such as the death of a parent or sibling, during their school years. It is estimated that each year about 15,000 pupils are bereaved of a parent in England and Wales. A study by Harrison and Harrington (2001) was based on questionnaires completed by 1746 pupils aged 11 to 16 years in the North of England. The percentages of bereavements they reported the pupils had experienced were as follows:

- parent: 4 per cent
- sibling: 5 per cent
- grandparent: 66 per cent
- uncle/aunt: 23 per cent
- close friend: 11 per cent
- treasured pet: 47 per cent
- other significant relative: 19 per cent.

They reported that the impact of the death on the pupil mainly depended on their perception of how the death had changed their lives. The loss of a parent or sibling was more strongly associated with depressive symptoms than was the case for other losses. Most of the pupils did not feel the need for professional services to help them cope with the bereavement.

Other types of loss akin to bereavement

An experience akin to bereavement can also be generated by other types of loss and change when a pupil is separated from someone or something they love and are emotionally attached to. The most common example of this is when parents separate or divorce. However, it can also be generated by other events, such as an older sibling leaving home, the family moving to another part of the country, which means leaving behind a group of very close friends, and even the relegation of the football team they support from the premier league. In all such cases, there are elements of grieving for the loss which has occurred, a wish that the clock could be turned back so that the event did not happen, and a recognition that one's life will have to adjust to the change. Depending on the precise circumstances, the strength of the emotional attachment involved, and, in particular, the nature of the events which follow (for example, whether a parent who has left the family home maintains regular contact), the time needed for adjustment can range from several weeks to several months (Atkinson and Hornby, 2002).

A study by Branwhite (1994) indicates just how common these different forms of loss can be. He asked 836 Year 7 pupils aged 11 to 12 years to consider a list of 14 events representing potential sources of social stress and to indicate for each one whether they had experienced the event and thought a lot about it afterwards. The percentage of pupils who responded 'yes' to the ones involving loss are as follows:

- losing a family pet because it died: 69 per cent
- losing a close relative because they died: 61 per cent
- moving house: 55 per cent
- having your parents split up: 26 per cent.

Effects on behaviour

The short-term effects on a pupil of experiencing a bereavement have been noted in a number of studies. For example, Holland and Ludford (1995) reported that the most common reactions noted by teachers were anger, depression, withdrawal, distress, attention seeking, reduced motivation, lack of concentration, and absenteeism.

There also appear to be long-term effects. For example, adults who become mentally ill, particularly with clinical depression, are more likely to have suffered a parental bereavement as a child than others. However, the long-term impact of bereavement can show itself more generally in terms of its impact on the person's subsequent view of the world.

Effects on personality

There are three areas where a bereavement can have effects on the development of a child's personality and the 'psychological baggage' they will carry with them into adulthood:

- *Emotional effects.* A person's ability to love and be loved by others involves risk – grief is the price you may have to pay for loving someone. A child may feel less willing to invest their love and be fully dependent on another person once they have experienced the pain of losing someone they love.

- *Cognitive effects.* The way the child views the bereavement will shape their view of the world; they may think, for example, that life must be viewed as essentially unpredictable, or lies in the hands of a 'powerful other' (such as God), or is simply subject to fate. As a result they may develop the view that people in life are powerless and helpless when it really matters, so there is no point in trying hard to shape what happens to you in your life or in struggling to overcome problems when the odds seem stacked against you.

- *Social effects.* The way a person relates to others can be affected by the feeling that life has dealt you a cruel hand, and that in some way 'it owes you one'; this may lead a pupil to become manipulative and self-centred in their social relationships.

Post-traumatic stress disorder

Kinchin and Brown (2001) point out that the crucial sign that a pupil may have been traumatised by the bereavement and be in need of therapeutic counselling may lie not so much in the severity of their response to the death, but rather in how long their reaction continues. A pupil is likely to be experiencing trauma, and possible post-traumatic stress disorder, if several months after the death they:

- are sad or depressed all the time
- are unable to engage in activities which interested them before the death
- express self-recrimination
- have become aggressive
- have become withdrawn
- experience flashbacks or nightmares
- pretend nothing has happened.

Death as a relief

It is also important to bear in mind that some pupils' reaction to a bereavement may be one of relief. For example, if a father who was abusive towards the rest of the family dies, the pupil might actually feel that the loss has improved their situation. Teachers therefore always need to be alert to the possibility that a pupil's reaction may not be as expected.

What can schools do to help pupils who suffer a bereavement?

Most teachers are unsure about how to respond to a pupil who is bereaved. In particular, they are not sure whether to take a reactive or a proactive stance. In the *reactive stance,* the teacher will simply carry on as normal, and wait to see if the pupil seems to want to talk about what has happened or is behaving in a way that suggests that some acknowledgement by the teacher about what has happened would be appropriate and helpful. In the *proactive stance*, the teacher will make the first move and tell the pupil they are very sorry to hear about the news, and that they should let them know if there is anything they can do to help.

Teachers involved in offering support to a pupil who has suffered a bereavement need to be sensitive to the religious and non-religious views held by the pupil's family. However, you may sometimes find it difficult to support what members of the family may have said to the pupil. Consequently you need to take care not to say things that may cause offence to the pupil's family, but at the same time also be careful not to condone views you may not agree with.

Dealing with a pupil who is bereaved can often be very upsetting for the teacher concerned. A study by Spall and Jordan (1999) of how 11 teachers reported helping pupils who had experienced a loss highlighted the personal distress experienced by the teachers. Their reactions included feeling inadequate about knowing how to help, initially wanting to avoid seeing the pupil, and feeling the pupil's hurt personally.

If the pupil seems to be reacting to the bereavement in a way that suggests they are finding it difficult to cope with everyday life and demands in the school, a gentle probing of their feelings would be in order to check whether the school can accommodate their needs better in any way. This might include considering in conjunction with a parent or parents whether counselling would be helpful. It is important to note here that the loss involves not only an emotional loss, but also changes to the pupil's material circumstances that the school needs to take account of. For example, the pupil may move house, money problems may start to occur, and the journey to school may be more difficult. The child's role in the family may also need to change. For example, an older sibling may have to take more responsibility for looking after their younger brother or sister, and helping out with various domestic tasks. This may lead to less time for homework and revision for tests and examinations, and attendance may also deteriorate.

The school's role when a bereavement is likely to occur

Schools can play an important role in helping pupils not only after a bereavement occurs but also in cases when a bereavement is expected, such as when a relative is seriously ill. In cases where a relative is seriously ill, this too can lead to changes in the pupil's life that might lead to them being late for school, not getting schoolwork done in time, and losing concentration and motivation in class. Much will also depend on how well the pupil is informed about the serious illness. Many parents find it difficult to tell their children when a relative is ill, and some feel that there is nothing served by telling a child that a relative may be dying. The school's main role here is to monitor the situation and accommodate the pupil's needs, and also to keep the parents informed if problems seem to be arising at school that are related to the pupil's fears or lack of information about whether a relative may be dying. The school may also need to be ready to alert parents to sources of support for them, as well as for the pupil, if a death does occur.

The school's role following a bereavement

When a death occurs, the school needs to express condolences to the family, to inform members of staff, and to contact the family to prepare for the pupil's return to school. Normally the pupil will learn of the bereavement from the family, but in certain circumstances a teacher may need to inform the pupil and escort the pupil home. Being told about the death of a loved one is clearly going to be a crucial moment in the pupil's life, and it needs to be done in a place where the pupil can be comforted and undisturbed. The school will also need to inform the pupil's friends and classmates.

If the death involves a brother or sister who was also a pupil at the school, or if it involves a teacher at the school, the whole school community will need to be informed, and arrangements will need to be made to acknowledge and commemorate the death, and for members of the school community to attend the funeral.

When the pupil returns to school, it is important for a senior member of staff in the school to offer condolences and support to the pupil. The pupil needs to be reassured that any changes in their behaviour, such as losing concentration and feeling upset, are a perfectly normal reaction, and that the grieving process will take some time. The pupil may also need help to catch up on work missed. If the pupil moves to another school soon after the bereavement, the new school needs to be informed about how the pupil is coping.

Schools also need to consider pupils' responses to the death of celebrities and prominent figures in society, such as pop idols, film stars and members of the royal family, and also the death of large numbers of people in a tragedy such as an accident or as a result of terrorism. The media coverage of such events can have an impact on pupils, and schools will sometimes wish to say something about such events during a school assembly.

Other agencies that can offer support

Holland (2000) interviewed senior teachers in 19 secondary schools in the North East of England regarding two types of loss suffered by pupils: the death of a parent and the separation of parents. All the teachers reported that the loss had a profound effect on the learning and behaviour of the pupil, but the effect depended on the individual and the context. Only 26 per cent of the schools had a formal procedure for dealing with a pupil's loss, and the others responded on an ad hoc basis. The agencies most frequently used by schools in giving support to pupils suffering loss were:

- educational psychologists
- educational welfare officers
- youth counsellors
- social workers
- Cruse (bereavement care) counsellors.

Bereavement counselling and support

Lines (2002) makes the point that the task of bereavement counselling is to help the pupil to understand and accept the loss, to be aware of the emotions that are experienced as part of the grieving process, and to encourage more adaptive behaviour. Pupils who are in need of therapeutic counselling will vary immensely in the aspect of the grieving process that they have become fixated on. For example, for one pupil it might be prolonged anger about the unfairness of the death and feelings of hostility towards everyone around them; for another it might be a sense of guilt that they had not been a better son or daughter, and that this is something they can now never put right.

There are a host of different approaches to therapeutic counselling, and the approach chosen will need to take careful account of the pupil's needs, age, and circumstances (Sharp and Cowie, 1998; Smith and Pennells, 1995). Of particular interest are the increasing number of approaches which make use of group activities.

Barnard *et al.* (1999) reported on a project working with pupils aged 6 to 12 years in Liverpool who had suffered a bereavement. They used a mixture of informal activities, which included talking, painting, drawing, music, drama and play, in small groups involving the pupils' closest friends and relatives to help them to explore their feelings. Barnard *et al.* argue that the key to helping pupils to deal with bereavement lies in enabling them to understand what has happened and to rediscover that they have a safe haven and dependable support.

Gisborne (1995) has described a grief support programme in Gloucestershire for bereaved pupils aged 5 to 14 years. The programme is based on eight principles:

- Grief is a natural reaction to the death of a significant person in both adults and children.
- Within each individual is the capacity to come to terms with life without the person who died.
- The duration and intensity of grief are unique for each individual.
- Caring and acceptance helps to facilitate the healing process.
- Children sometimes find it difficult to express their thoughts and feelings about death to close family members.

- Meeting other children who have shared similar experiences helps to improve a bereaved child's self-esteem.
- The reaction of a child's living parent has a fundamental effect on the child's own grief process.
- Unresolved childhood grief can lead to behavioural, emotional or educational difficulties.

When a pupil is referred to as being in need of support, an individual assessment and home visit is made to assess the needs of the pupil, who is then offered one of three entry points:

- individual support
- after-school group
- Camp Winston.

The most common entry point is Camp Winston, which is a two-day residential camp at a country house. At the same time the parents and carers are offered their own two-day non-residential camp which coincides with Camp Winston. The focus at both camps is on therapeutic rituals and exercises which aim to encourage people to talk openly about death and express their feelings. The core team involved in this work have links with schools and advise and support teachers in dealing with a bereavement.

Le Count (2000) notes that although children need to be able to work through their grief, they all too often hold back their questions and feelings for fear of upsetting adults close to them. She describes how creative art therapy using drawing, painting and modelling with clay can help such pupils acknowledge and release their feelings about a bereavement.

Melvin and Lukeman (2000) note that pupils suffering from a bereavement are likely to be in the care of adults who are also grieving. Consequently the adults may require support themselves in order to help them offer support to the pupil. Melvin and Lukeman also list six factors that can play an important role in protecting pupils from immediate and long-term disturbance following a bereavement:

- *Child.* It helps if the child has the ability to form an internal image of the dead person and can retain a memory or link with that person.
- *Parent.* It helps if a replacement figure can fill in some of the role that the dead person had in the care of the child in terms of both practical and emotional needs; this is especially the case if it is the mother who has died. It also helps if the surviving parent had a good prior relationship with the child and is not overwhelmed by their own grief.
- *Family.* It helps if family roles are flexible and there is a good level of communication within the family; it also helps if there are no other major transitions and changes in the family's situation or lifestyle.
- *Friends.* It helps if contact with friends can be maintained; friends often provide the main support network in the case of older pupils.

- *School*. It helps if the school provides easy access to individual support, and the school has open discussions about life and death.

- *Community*. It helps if there are role models in the local community who can explain the behaviour and rituals surrounding a death.

Staff training

The need for staff training has been noted in a number of studies (Bowie, 2000; Eiser *et al.*, 1995). There are two aspects to such training: firstly, to help teachers in their role of providing support to a pupil who has experienced a bereavement; secondly, to help teachers to teach death education. Whilst the vast majority of teachers express the view that training regarding the former would be welcomed, teachers' views about the latter are somewhat mixed, and some teachers are unconvinced that death education would be either worthwhile or appropriate.

Is there a role for death education to help prepare pupils to deal with bereavement in the future?

The assumption is often made that the vast majority of pupils rarely think about death unless the death of someone they know occurs. However, various studies indicate that many pupils often think about death. Indeed, it is one of the areas of cognitive and emotional development that all children gradually need to come to terms with. For example, a study by Bowie (2000) asked 107 primary school pupils in Scotland aged 9 to 11 years 'Is death and dying a topic which you think about?' She reported that on a three-point scale, 31 per cent replied 'quite a lot', 42 per cent replied 'sometimes' and 27 per cent replied 'never'. Nevertheless, there is an important distinction to be made between 'thinking about death' as an abstract concept that they need to understand and incorporate into their view of the world, and the personal worries that may stem from the death of someone they know.

Death education in the school curriculum

The most common areas of the school curriculum which include activities dealing with bereavement are religious education, PSHE and English.

Clark (1998) in reviewing death education in the UK focused on four strands:

- informing of facts not currently widespread in society
- dealing with feelings about one's own death and the death of significant others
- becoming informed consumers of medical and funeral services
- clarifying one's values regarding social and ethical issues.

A study by Rowling and Holland (2000) compared education about loss and grief at 46 secondary schools in England and 48 secondary school in New South Wales, Australia. In Australia, 29 per cent of the schools reported including this in their school curriculum, whereas in England only 9 per cent of the schools did so. The main aim of education about loss and grief in both countries was for pupils to recognise 'loss and grief as a life experience'.

The central task for the school curriculum in dealing with death and bereavement in the primary school years is to look in more general terms at the impact that change has on people, and to include within this the impact of death and bereavement. This will enable primary school pupils to consider how individuals might react to a death which occurs in the family and the consequences this might have for those affected. In the secondary school years, the treatment of death and bereavement would be extended to consider issues such as the grieving process, how bereaved people cope with their loss, and how a bereaved person may need support. A number of programmes also include looking specifically at the nature and purpose of funerals in helping individuals to acknowledge a death. Such activities can make use of a wide range of literature, including stories, plays and poems, as well as material specifically produced to raise issues concerning death.

Leaman (1995) notes that there are a few countries, such as the United States, where death education is quite widespread, and in some secondary schools death education features as a mainstream school curriculum course in its own right. Such courses typically include:

- historical and cultural background
- thoughts and feelings about death
- death, loss, separation and grief as related ideas
- dying
- bereavement
- suicide
- death education
- counselling issues
- consumer issues.

In a study which involved visits to 43 schools in England to explore children's perceptions of death and reactions to loss, Leaman highlights a number of ethical issues and sensitivities facing teachers involved in death education. He points out that whilst at any one time most of the class will be treating the topic in hand in general terms, there may be some pupils in the class who have experienced a bereavement. The teacher therefore needs to be aware at all times that some pupils' reactions to the topic may be affected by their personal experience, and that the questions pupils ask may be related to trying to make sense of the personal experiences they are still working through. For example, during a visit to a museum to look at Ancient Egyptian mummies, one girl asked the teacher whether the beliefs the Ancient Egyptians held about an after-life would apply to her father who had died. During this visit, the teacher appeared to be uncomfortable in handling questions from some pupils about things which were of direct concern to them and continually tried to steer the discussion back to the beliefs held by the Ancient Egyptians and the rituals involved. In death education, a teacher will often experience this type of tension between looking at death as a general topic and looking at death as a means to explore pupils' personal experiences of death.

It is also interesting to note that at times of war, schools may be issued with guidance on how death education can best be addressed within the school curriculum. It is not clear whether this is simply a recognition of the information needs of pupils that will follow from media attention to the deaths which occur during such hostilities, or whether it is also intended to help pupils to prepare for the death of someone they know who is in the armed forces. Similar issues also arise in the context of regional hostilities, where terrorism has increased the need for death education (such as in Northern Ireland, Israel or the Basque region of Spain).

A number of writers have produced texts which will help teachers to develop materials and activities to teach about death (e.g. Jackson and Colwell, 2001). Some of the topics involved can be taught through PSHE or religious education, whilst others can be taught as part of curriculum areas such as English, art and history. However, it is important that teachers who cover such topics are aware of the personal sensitivities which may be involved. For example, a lesson which involves looking at funerals may serve to remind a pupil that they did not attend the funeral of their parent who died a few years ago, and that might in retrospect elicit the anxiety and lack of closure that some people feel if they did not attend the funeral of someone they loved.

There is little doubt that the idea of death education is controversial, and that some parents may have strong views about whether it should be taught and, if so, what ideas should be covered and how. In addition, there are sensitivities here concerning the age of the pupils and also the type of religious and non-religious views that may be held. Those schools which decide to offer death education will therefore need to ensure that the teaching is handled with extreme care, and parents and staff will need to be involved in consenting to what is offered.

ACTION POINTS

School policy on bereavement support

All schools need to have a policy on bereavement support which details the action to be taken when a pupil suffers a bereavement. In particular, at least one member of staff needs to be designated to monitor the situation and the pupil's needs, to convey condolences to the pupil and to offer to talk to the pupil whenever needed. All teachers and the pupil's classmates also need to be informed. The policy might include guidance for teachers on their role, and a list of do's and don'ts. The policy also needs to include a note of the role of outside agencies that can offer support if and when needed.

Pastoral support for a bereaved pupil

The person designated to monitor the pupil's reaction and needs should be proactive on more than one occasion. Even in the case of a pupil who seems to be coping well, the teacher should check with them a couple of weeks following the bereavement how things are going. This role requires great sensitivity that takes account of the individual pupil's needs, their context and circumstances. As well as addressing their emotional reaction, the teacher needs to check that the pupil's practical needs are addressed.

Information support for a bereaved pupil

Young pupils in particular may have information needs concerning the death. Some of these are best addressed by the pupil's family. Nevertheless a teacher may be asked questions that are difficult to answer, such as 'Has Mum gone to heaven?' or 'Is it my fault that Dad died?' Care needs to be taken to ensure that nothing is said that can cause confusion.

Counselling

Teachers need to be aware of the signs that a pupil may be in need of additional support and, in some cases, therapeutic counselling. It is important that teachers are alert to when outside agencies need to be involved rather than attempting to address more complex needs themselves.

Staff training

All teachers need to receive some basic guidance on how to help a bereaved pupil. At the very least, this should involve a briefing session on the contents of the school policy documents. When a bereavement occurs, the teachers closest to the pupil could usefully receive an information sheet of do's and don'ts regarding their role.

School policy on crises

All schools should have a policy on how to react when a tragedy occurs affecting pupils at the school, such as the death of a pupil or a teacher on school premises or a major accident involving pupils. This will need to deal with what decisions need to be taken and by whom, and to include a list of the outside agencies that need to be involved.

Death education

The role of death education here is to prepare pupils to cope with a bereavement by making them more familiar with the nature of death, the rituals that take place, the likely feelings of those involved, the mourning process, and the changes that may follow for members of the immediate family. Death education can do much to reduce the level of confusion that can occur following a death, and also help a pupil to appreciate what feelings can be expected. In the long term, death education can also help pupils when they become parents themselves to play a role in supporting their own children following a bereavement. Nevertheless, death education is a controversial area, and schools offering it need to do so with great sensitivity and with the consent of the teachers and parents.

References

Atkinson, M. and Hornby, G. (2002) *Mental Health Handbook for Schools*. London: RoutledgeFalmer.

Barnard, P., Morland, I. and Nagy, J. (1999) *Children, Bereavement and Trauma: Nurturing Resilience*. London: Jessica Kingsley.

Bowie, L. (2000) 'Is there a place for death in the primary curriculum?' *Pastoral Care in Education*, 18(1), 22–6.

Branwhite, T. (1994) 'Bullying and student distress: beneath the tip of the iceberg.' *Educational Psychology*, 14(1), 59–71.

Brown, E. (1999) *Loss, Change and Grief: An Educational Perspective*. London: David Fulton.

Clark, V. (1998) 'Death education in the United Kingdom.' *Journal of Moral Education*, 27(3), 393–400.

Eiser, C., Havermans, T., Rolph, P. and Rolph, J. (1995) 'The place of bereavement and loss in the curriculum: teachers' attitudes.' *Pastoral Care in Education*, 13(4), 32–6.

Gisborne, T. (1995) 'Death and bereavement in school: are you prepared?' *Education 3–13*, 23(2), 39–44.

Gudas, L. S. and Koocher, G. P. (2001) 'Children with grief.' In C. E. Walker and M. C. Roberts (eds) *Handbook of Clinical Child Psychology*, 3rd edn (pp. 1046–56). Chichester: Wiley.

Harrison, L. and Harrington, R. (2001) 'Adolescents' bereavement experiences: prevalence, association with depressive symptoms and use of services.' *Journal of Adolescence*, 24(2), 159–69.

Holland, J. M. (1997) *Coping with Bereavement: A Handbook for Teachers*. Cardiff: Cardiff Academic Press.

Holland, J. M. (2000) 'Secondary schools and pupil loss by parental bereavement and parental relationship separations.' *Pastoral Care in Education*, 18(4), 33–9.

Holland, J. M. (2001) *Understanding Children's Experiences of Parental Bereavement*. London: Jessica Kingsley.

Holland, J. M. and Ludford, C. (1995) 'The effects of bereavement on children in Humberside secondary schools.' *British Journal of Special Education*, 22(2), 56–9.

Jackson, M. and Colwell, J. (2001) *A Teacher's Handbook of Death*. London: Jessica Kingsley.

Kinchin, D. and Brown, E. (2001) *Supporting Children with Post-traumatic Stress Disorder: A Practical Guide for Teachers and Professionals*. London: David Fulton.

Leaman, O. (1995) *Death and Loss: Compassionate Approaches in the Classroom.* London: Cassell.

Le Count, D. (2000) 'Working with 'difficult' children from the inside out: loss and bereavement and how the creative arts can help.' *Pastoral Care in Education*, 18(2), 17–27.

Lines, D. (2002) *Brief Counselling in Schools.* London: Sage.

Mallon, B. (1998) *Helping Children to Manage Loss: Positive Strategies for Renewal and Growth.* London: Jessica Kingsley.

Melvin, D. and Lukeman, D. (2000) 'Bereavement: a framework for those working with children.' *Clinical Child Psychology and Psychiatry*, 5(4), 521–39.

Renzenbrink, I. (2002) 'Children's responses to the death of a grandparent.' *Bereavement Care*, 21(1), 6–8.

Rowling, J. and Holland, J. (2000) 'Grief and school communities: the impact of social context, a comparison between Australia and England.' *Death Studies*, 24(1), 35–50.

Sharp, S. and Cowie, H. (1998) *Counselling and Supporting Children in Distress.* London: Sage.

Smith, S. C. and Pennells, M. (eds) (1995) *Interventions with Bereaved Children.* London: Jessica Kingsley.

Spall, B. and Jordan, G. (1999) 'Teachers' perspectives on working with children experiencing loss.' *Pastoral Care in Education*, 17(3), 3–7.

Wagner, P. (1995) 'Schools and pupils: developing their responses to bereavement.' In R. Best, P. Lang, C. Lodge and C. Watkins (eds) *Pastoral Care and Personal-Social Education: Entitlement and Provision* (pp. 204–22). London: Cassell.

9 Delinquency

Criminal acts committed by youngsters are a major cause for concern, not only because they may be symptomatic of troubled youth, but also because of the immense pain and suffering they can cause for their families and for the victims of these crimes. At a time when youngsters should be looking forward to the positive possibilities that life has to offer them during adulthood, it is sobering and a source of despair that many youngsters, even before approaching the latter years of their schooling, already seem to have embarked on a life of crime and anti-social behaviour. Whatever the personal and social factors might be that encourage pupils to commit crimes, schools can play a crucial role in counteracting them, by encouraging pupils to develop pro-social behaviour and to feel positive about themselves and their future prospects.

What do we mean by 'juvenile delinquency' and how common is it?

Juvenile delinquency is defined as committing an illegal offence between the ages of 10 (the age of criminal responsibility in England and Wales) and 17 years, although much discussion of delinquency also includes those aged 18 to 20 years who are strictly speaking defined as young adults or young offenders. Youths under the age of 21 years account for about 45 per cent of all convictions in England and Wales each year. The peak for delinquency appears to be around 16 years for males and 15 years for females. Approximately 6 per cent of male juveniles will have been convicted of at least one offence before the age of 17 years. Only a small minority of delinquents go on to have criminal careers as adults. The majority of convictions involve theft, burglary and handling stolen goods, and only about 10 per cent involve violence (Croall, 1998; Muncie, 1999).

Estimating the incidence of delinquency

Statistics about juvenile delinquency need to be treated with great caution, because many offences which are committed go unreported, many of those which are reported go unrecorded, and many of those which are recorded do not lead to a conviction. Figures based on recorded crime and convictions will therefore only represent a small proportion of the crimes which have actually been committed. As a result, many studies have sought to use self-reported measures of criminal activity to gain a better estimate of the level of actual delinquency which occurs. However, such studies suffer from difficulties in obtaining a valid and representative sample, and the self-reports themselves can be subject to bias and inflation.

A survey of anti-social behaviour and youth crime reported by Beinart *et al.* (2002) was based on a questionnaire completed by 14,445 secondary school pupils aged 11 to 16 years in England, Scotland and Wales. The authors reported that 49 per cent of the pupils admitted breaking the law at least once, as evidenced by offences such as stealing, criminal damage, shoplifting, carrying a weapon, attacking someone with the intention of causing them serious harm, and selling drugs. The percentage of pupils admitting criminal activities in Years 7 and 11 is shown in Table 9.1.

Table 9.1   Percentages of pupils admitting criminal activities in Years 7 and 11

Criminal activity	Year 7 (11–12 year olds)	Year 11 (15–16 year olds)
Had ever stolen or tried to steal something	20	41
Had vandalised property during the past year	11	28
Had shoplifted during the past year	9	23
Carried a weapon	6	16
Had attacked someone, intending to harm them	6	14
Had sold or dealt illegal drugs	1	9

Source: Beinart et al. (2002)

More crimes were committed by pupils in Years 10 and 11 (aged 14 to 16 years) than by pupils in Years 7 to 9 (aged 11 to 14 years). More boys than girls committed crimes in Years 7 to 9. The gender gap decreased in Years 10 and 11 for vandalism and shoplifting, but not for violent behaviour or more serious crimes. In Year 11, 24 per cent of the boys said they had carried a weapon to school or in the street during the past year and 19 per cent of boys had attacked someone else intending to seriously harm them. Serious property crimes, such as burglary and theft, were less common and were admitted by older boys. For example, 10 per cent of boys in Year 11 said they had broken into a building to steal during the previous year, including 4 per cent who said they had done so three times or more.

The percentages of pupils drinking alcohol, smoking and taking illegal drugs also increased steadily between Years 7 and 11. By Year 11, 80 per cent of pupils had drunk alcohol in the previous four weeks, 16 per cent were regular smokers, and 7 per cent had used cannabis on three or more occasions in the previous four weeks.

The authors noted that the survey indicated that most of the pupils were law abiding most of the time, but that the findings in respect of the levels of violence and under-age alcohol consumption reported were particularly worrying. A large majority of the pupils agreed that there were clear rules at home and their parents would think it wrong for them to steal or use illegal drugs.

Risk factors and protective factors

The report by Beinart *et al.* also describes 17 risk factors and five protective factors for delinquency derived from analysis of, mainly, longitudinal research studies and chosen because they appear susceptible to modification by a community-based programme (see Table 9.2). The protective factors were linked to positive outcomes even when children were growing up in adverse circumstances and heavily exposed to risk.

Table 9.2   Risk factors and protective factors for juvenile delinquency

Risk factors	Protective factors
Family • Poor parental supervision and discipline • Family conflict • Family history of problem behaviour • Parental involvement/attitudes condoning problem behaviour • Low income and poor housing **School** • Low achievement, beginning at primary school • Aggressive behaviour, including bullying • Lack of commitment, including truancy • School disorganisation **Community** • Community disorganisation and neglect • Availability of drugs • Disadvantaged neighbourhood • High turnover and lack of neighbourhood attachment **Individuals, friends and peers** • Alienation and lack of social commitment • Attitudes that condone problem behaviour • Early involvement in problem behaviour • Involvement of friends in problem behaviour	• Strong bonds with family, friends and teachers • Healthy standards set by parents, teachers and community leaders • Opportunities for involvement in families, schools and the community • Social and learning skills to enable participation • Recognition and praise for positive behaviour

Source: Beinart et al. (2000)

A distinction is often made between the occasional petty crimes committed by some youths, and a smaller group of persistent offenders who commit large numbers of crimes and are sometimes referred to as being 'beyond control'. Studies focusing on persistent offenders indicate that they are more likely to have chaotic lives and to have had more frequent contact with social services. However, studies of persistent offenders need to be looked at with caution because persistence (i.e. frequent offending) should not be confused with serious offences, which are still relatively rare amongst juveniles.

Types of delinquents

Delinquents are much more likely to be male, the ratio of males to females varying for different types of offences. In the case of taking and driving away motor vehicles the ratio is about 33:1, for robbery about 14:1 and for drug offences about 9:1. Afro-Caribbean youths are also over-represented, although the extent of this is unclear as official statistics often do not record ethnic origin, and what figures do exist are not corrected to take account of socio-economic circumstances.

Given the variety of different crimes committed by delinquents, a number of writers have argued that a full understanding of delinquency may need to take account of different categories of crime and the subcultures that give rise to these. For example, one useful distinction that has been made is between the following three main kinds of delinquent subcultures (Croall, 1998):

- a *conflict* subculture characterised by fighting, violence and 'gang warfare'
- a *criminal* subculture characterised by organised crime and the associated illegitimate sale of the proceeds of property crime
- a *retreatist* subculture characterised by truancy, drug taking and heavy drinking.

It is important to note, however, that some writers, such as Gottfredson (2001), use the term juvenile delinquency to refer to a broader range of problem behaviour, which includes arriving late for lessons, swearing at the teacher and cheating in examinations. Gottfredson makes that point that restricting the term simply to illegal acts is artificial since non-criminal problem behaviour is behaviourally analogous to criminal behaviour in its causation. However, my view is that restricting the term to criminal acts is important, because there is a line that most pupils themselves recognise within problem behaviour between what is non-criminal and what is criminal, and it is important to understand those factors that contribute specifically to the latter.

What are the causes and types of juvenile delinquency?

Some writers see delinquency as merely the expression of a general malaise in youth culture whereby many adolescents have failed to learn definite moral standards from their parents, are hedonistic, easily bored, contemptuous of the law and easily led astray by their peers. Such an analysis, whilst frequently expressed in the media, is a gross over-simplification and bears little relation to the fact that the vast majority of adolescents are well behaved, have a clear sense of morality and are respectful of authority.

Factors influencing persistent offending

Three factors that appear to be common amongst persistent offenders are *emotional coldness*, *normalisation to a criminal subculture* and *problems with impulse control* (Johnson and Shaw, 2001).

Persistent offenders often grow up in a household where they have experienced trauma, physical violence, inconsistent discipline, parental disharmony and a lack of care, and this has had the effect of brutalising them to some extent. As a result, they are less sympathetic and less able to have compassion for the victims of their crimes. This is best described as an emotional coldness, which results in their having little inhibition about committing criminal acts compared with others. This emotional coldness can sometimes be turned inwards on themselves, and displays itself in an apparent lack of concern about what might happen to them if they are caught and punished.

Persistent offenders also often grow up in a household where they become aware of criminal activities committed by those around them, either by members of their own family or by their friends and others that they associate with in their local community. As a result, they become normalised to accepting crime as a normal acceptable activity within the framework of their immediate reference group.

Persistent offenders also often have problems with impulse control – they are unable or unwilling to curb natural impulses to pursue pleasure or to relieve sources of irritation. Persistent offenders often complain that they were simply unable to control their urges or resist the temptations offered to them to gain from criminal activity. Indeed, persistent offenders often come to rationalise that it is fair for them to act in this way, because the harshness and deprived nature of their upbringing and home circumstances meant that 'society' in some way owed them a better lifestyle that they were now entitled to claim for themselves even if they had to do so illegally.

The above three risk factors serve to increase markedly the likelihood that a youth will commit criminal acts. Other risk factors include poverty, living in a single-parent household, having a close relative who has been convicted of criminal activity, and having an aggressive personality. As the number of risk factors that apply to a given individual increases, the likelihood of that individual committing a crime increases. Awareness of such risk factors can sometimes be used to target young children at risk of crime and thereby provide them with, or make available in their local community, activities and experiences that might help them to resist the temptations of crime. Examples would be the provision of youth centres and sports facilities in such communities.

However, there are still a number of imponderables here. It needs to be born in mind that some pupils exposed to such risk factors do not become persistent offenders, and that some pupils who are not exposed to such risk factors do become persistent offenders. This serves to highlight the complexity of the way in which different aspects of a child's upbringing and circumstances may interact in order either to predispose them to commit a crime or to help them to resist committing a crime.

In addition, crime can sometimes be prompted by bravado and pleasure seeking, whereby the individuals themselves might not feel the incidents really constitute what they would regard as criminal behaviour. Incidents of criminal damage, such as smashing up a telephone box, being drunk and disorderly, assaulting others during an argument, joyriding and the use of drugs, are regarded by some adolescents simply as sensation seeking – as bad behaviour rather than criminal. They would draw a distinction between such behaviour and the premeditated crimes such as burglary, pickpocketing and fraud. Whilst a crime is defined with strict reference to the law, every individual draws a line between criminal behaviour which they would regard as an acceptable occasional transgression on their part and criminal behaviour which they would never dream of being engaged in. This distinction reflects their own moral values and attitudes. Just as some 'law abiding' adults view shortchanging an honesty box, breaking the speed limit and taking things home that belong to one's employer as trivial acts, some 'law abiding' juveniles take a similar view of smoking cannabis, shoplifting and fare dodging.

The delinquent trajectory

A study by Cullingford (1999), based on interviews with 25 young people aged 16 to 21 years who were currently in institutions for young offenders, highlights the track that many delinquents follow, which starts with things going wrong in their early years at home, such as having parents who did not seem to be bothered with them, family breakdown and dysfunction, and suffering violence and abuse. The school years are then typically characterised by getting into trouble on a regular basis, developing a violent temper they are unable to control, being involved in bullying, and being excluded from school. Juvenile delinquency is the final outcome of this track, and a manifestation of the feelings of dysfunction and social exclusion they experienced throughout their childhood. Cullingford and Morrison (1995) note the extent to which this group saw bullying and fighting at school as a normal aspect of the school ethos, and their experience of bullying (either as a bully or as a victim) as 'normal behaviour' creates a mental culture which is linked to the development of subsequent criminality. Cullingford and Morrison (1997) note the way in which the exclusion that such pupils experienced both at home and at school results in both the home and the school being unable to exert an influence on these pupils to avoid engaging in crime, and they are then very vulnerable to the influence of deviant peers.

The Social Exclusion Unit (1998) has also highlighted the link between truancy, exclusion and delinquency. Approximately half of all school-aged offenders have been excluded from school and about a quarter have truanted significantly. Truants are about three times more likely to offend than non-truants. It has also been estimated that about 5 per cent of all offences are committed by children during school hours.

Problems of emotion control

The notion that pupils who find it difficult to control their emotions might be prone to delinquency has been explored in a number of studies. Research on coping with stress indicates that stress can be heightened for those people who tend to rehearse emotionally upsetting events. Roger (1997) notes that this has led to two ideas concerning a link between poor emotion control and offending behaviour. The first idea is that poor emotion control leads to frustration and anger thereby resulting in violent behaviour. The second idea is that offending behaviour can be encouraged in those who derive excitement from committing crimes, and who then experience further excitement before or after a crime by mentally rehearsing the behaviour, thereby experiencing vicarious gratification. Indeed, delinquents often talk of the intense buzz and excitement they derive from criminal activity. It has been argued that those with a tendency to ruminate about their crimes may through the impact of vicarious gratification become addicted to committing further crimes, particularly crimes involving sex offending, where fantasising about the crime can play a key part in reinforcing the cycle of offending. This analysis would indicate that the childhood experiences of pupils who develop poor emotion-control strategies may make them vulnerable to delinquency, and that intervention strategies aimed at delinquents or those at risk of delinquency could usefully focus on helping them to develop greater emotion control, particularly through anger-management strategies and the avoidance of emotional rumination.

Links with drug abuse

Some writers have argued that there is such a strong link between drug abuse and crime that we can refer to a 'delinquency syndrome' comprising these two behaviours and use a single model to identify a single set of underlying problems which leads to both elements of the syndrome. In order to explore this idea, Benda and Corwyn (2000) looked at the behaviour of 387 adolescents aged 12 to 18 years in a Mid-Western state of the United States. They found that whilst most factors indeed correlated significantly with both admitted frequency of crime and use of drugs, there were four factors which were more strongly correlated with crime than with use of drugs. These were:

- *Beliefs.* Those who committed crimes had less belief in the moral validity of social laws and norms.
- *Parental abuse.* Those who committed crimes reported more physical abuse from parents.
- *Excuses.* Those who committed crimes were more willing to rationalise excuses for their behaviour.
- *Peer association.* Those who committed crimes felt they had close friends who would not think less of them if they committed crimes.

They concluded that whilst crime and drug abuse were commonly related, the trajectories that lead to these two types of criminal behaviour are likely to be different in important respects.

Identifying at-risk pupils

A number of studies have attempted to identify pupils at risk of becoming juvenile delinquents, with a view to targeting interventions with such pupils. In general, the best predictor of future behaviour is current behaviour. For example, the pupils most likely to become delinquents are pupils who persistently misbehaved and were regarded as troublemakers in primary schools. Even in the pre-school years, their parents often remarked they were hard to control and often got into mischief.

Carroll *et al.* (1999) argue that a key factor in identifying primary school pupils at risk of having problems later in their school careers relates to the development of their goal orientations and how they perceive their social reputation. In a study of 886 primary school pupils aged 10 to 12 years in Brisbane, Australia, they identified pupils as being at risk using a checklist of 12 behavioural indicators and 12 situational indicators, shown in Table 9.3, which were completed by the pupils' classroom teachers.

Table 9.3 Indicators used to identify primary school pupils at risk of having problems later in their school careers

Behavioural indicators	Situational indicators
Truanting	Suspended
Disruptive	Expelled
Self-harm	In time-out rooms
Anti-social	Incarcerated
Violent	Welfare
Rejection of teacher support	Homeless
Rejection of parent support	Social disadvantage
Stealing	Family breakdown
Vandalism	Transient family
Arson	Parental unemployment
Drug use	Abused
Poor motivation	Poor socio-economic status

Source: Carroll et al. (1999)

On this basis about 13 per cent of the sample were identified as being at risk (comprising four times as many boys as girls). The pupils completed a questionnaire which explored their perceptions about their goals and social reputations. The at-risk

134

pupils were significantly more likely to have 'delinquent goals' than the pupils who were not at risk. The at-risk pupils admired law-breaking activities, such as bullying, smoking cigarettes, truancy and stealing money; they perceived themselves and wished to be perceived by others as bad kids, troublemakers, bullies, breaking rules, doing things against the law and getting into trouble with the police. These findings indicate that the quest by at-risk pupils to seek and attain a delinquent reputation often begins at the primary school.

Longitudinal research on delinquency

A very important longitudinal study of juvenile delinquency is the Cambridge Study in Delinquent Development undertaken by Farrington (1995, 1999, 2000). This study is based on a sample of 411 working-class boys selected in 1961 at the age of 8 or 9 years who attended primary schools in Camberwell, London. They have since been followed up at regular intervals to identify which boys became delinquents. About a fifth of the sample committed crimes as juveniles, but only about 6 per cent of the sample (23 men) became chronic offenders in adulthood. Farrington identified six variables as predictors of future criminality:

- anti-social child behaviour
- hyperactivity, impulsivity and attention deficit
- low intelligence and poor school attainment
- family criminality
- family poverty
- poor parental child-rearing behaviour.

In addition, those convicted at an early age (10–13 years) tended to become the most persistent offenders. The best predictor of a pupil becoming a chronic adult offender was having a convicted parent before the age of 10 years.

Another important longitudinal study is the Dunedin Multidisciplinary Health and Development Study based on 1037 children born in Dunedin, New Zealand (Moffitt, 1993; Moffitt *et al.*, 2001). These children were first assessed in 1975 at the age of 3 years. In an analysis of juvenile delinquency amongst the boys in this cohort, Moffitt identified two distinct groups. The first group comprises boys who exhibited anti-social behaviour throughout their childhood and adolescence. This group were labelled *life-course-persistent delinquents* and accounted for about 5 per cent of the boys. The second group only began to exhibit anti-social behaviour during adolescence and stopped thereafter. These were labelled *adolescence-limited delinquents* and accounted for about a third of the boys. Moffitt argues that most of the delinquency amongst the second group arose through social mimicry of the first group, and that a number of the pupils in this first group may well be suffering from a neurobiological problem. An analysis of delinquent girls in this cohort indicated that life-course-persistent delinquency is uncommon in girls, most of whom fit the adolescence-limited pattern.

The data also point to the greater prevalence of delinquency amongst males as indicated by both self-reported offences and court records. For example, youth aid police records indicated that 20 per cent of the males had been contacted by the police between the ages of 10 and 16 years compared with 10 per cent of the females.

A particularly interesting finding was that female delinquency in later adolescence was strongly exacerbated when females partnered with delinquent males. Moffitt reported that delinquent girls were more likely to become involved with male criminals and that this then led to further crime. Moffitt argues that partnering criminal men plays a key role in women's transition from juvenile delinquency to adult crime.

These two longitudinal studies both highlight the distinction between a small proportion of boys who seem to be in trouble throughout their childhood and who become persistent offenders, and a much larger proportion of boys who seem to get into trouble only for a short period during their adolescence, and whose criminality seems to be a temporary form of experimentation largely encouraged by some of their peers. These findings are also in line with the estimate that about 5 per cent of delinquents account for about 50 per cent of the crimes committed by juveniles.

Those who stop being delinquent

A study by Graham and Bowling (1995) was based on questionnaires completed by 2529 subjects aged 14 to 25 years. The study indicated, in line with other research, that offending was higher amongst those who did not like school, whose work at school was of a lower standard, who truanted, who were excluded, and who had friends that were in trouble with the police. An analysis of the data in terms of three age groups (14–17, 18–21 and 22–25) indicated a steady decline in the total amount of self-reported offending with age, with the figure for the 22–25-year-old group being 23 per cent lower than for the 14–17-year-old group. The study also asked those who had committed an offence whether they would do so again. About two-thirds said they would not. The main reasons given for not committing an offence again were:

- it's childish (25 per cent)
- the risk of getting caught (20 per cent)
- it's wrong (15 per cent)
- my life has changed (9 per cent)
- it's pointless (8 per cent).

Graham and Bowling make the point that most delinquents grow out of crime, but that many people, even by their mid-twenties, have still not completed the transition to a fully independent adult life, and that the period of adolescence has lengthened markedly over the last 50 years. In order to explore 'desistance' further, they identified a groups of 'desisters', who were categorised as those who had committed three or more relatively serious offences at some point in the past, but had not committed any offences within the past year. A total of 166 subjects were identified as desisters. The study then conducted life-history interviews with a sample of 21 of these and identified four processes which appear to influence desistance from offending:

- dissociation from delinquent peers
- forming stable relationships and having children
- acquiring a sense of direction
- realising in time or learning the hard way.

What can schools do to help 'at risk' pupils and reduce juvenile delinquency?

Perhaps the most important role a school can play in combating juvenile delinquency is helping pupils to achieve well academically and socialising the pupil into behaving well. Schools which are successful in promoting academic achievement and good behaviour are already doing much to reduce the level of youth crime. An important element in their success is a whole-school policy promoting good behaviour, which is marked by three essential features:

- clear agreement amongst all staff in the school regarding the standards of behaviour expected of pupils, and the procedures to be followed where there is a cause for concern
- a recognition that all staff must act consistently and as a team in line with the agreed school policy, and must collaborate and be mutually supportive in addressing how best to deal with discipline problems
- the adoption of a set of actions that the school can take, including, for example, the use of praise in the classroom or a merit system for good work and good behaviour, and the use of aspects of the school's PSHE programme which aim to positively promote good behaviour rather than simply react when poor behaviour occurs.

Intervention in early childhood

Mendel (2001) notes that the most effective delinquency-prevention programme is early childhood education. An interesting aspect of the 'Head Start' pre-school programmes in the United States, which aimed to combat school failure amongst pupils from disadvantaged communities, was that those programmes which were successful in raising pupils' later school achievement were also successful in reducing the incidence of juvenile delinquency. The effectiveness of such programmes is twofold. Firstly, school success of itself will help raise self-esteem and enable pupils to assume roles in society that will gain them the respect of adults, and this makes such pupils less vulnerable to peer-group pressure to engage in crime. Secondly, school success will reduce the risk of truancy, exclusion and dropping out, which play an important role in the trajectory towards juvenile crime.

Combating exclusion

The particular challenge that faces schools is to keep on board pupils who are at risk of exclusion, and the action outlined in chapter 5 on reducing the likelihood of exclusion will also be of key importance in reducing juvenile delinquency. Indeed, a number of school-based projects aimed at reducing juvenile delinquency are successful largely by reducing exclusions and thereby breaking the trajectory that leads from misbehaviour to exclusion to delinquency.

For example, a project evaluated by Webb and Vulliamy (2002) involved home–school support workers working in seven secondary schools in York and North Yorkshire over a three-year period. The support provided by the support workers to 208 caseload pupils involved:

- befriending
- offering ongoing counselling and support
- individual approaches and group work related to areas such as anger management, self-esteem and relationships with peers
- advocacy and mediation
- advice on personal, social and health problems
- referral to other agencies.

The support workers also tried out a number of development activities such as a drugs evening for parents and workshops for teachers on counselling pupils. The evaluation indicated that the project had led to a 25 per cent reduction in the permanent exclusions amongst the caseload pupils.

Avoiding the effects of labelling

A number of writers have pointed to the powerful effects of labelling on pupils' self-perceptions, and how once pupils come into conflict with authority (teachers and the police) they start to see themselves as troublemakers. This then creates a vicious circle in which they engage in further misbehaviour, in part because they feel it is the behaviour they and others have now come to expect of themselves. It is thus very important that teachers make every effort to distinguish clearly in their dealings with a pupil between the person and the person's behaviour. The message that teachers need to get across to pupils who are at risk of exclusion or who have committed a crime is that it is their behaviour that is causing the problem, and that with the school's support and encouragement they want to help the pupil to behave better in future. In trying to side with the person and to help distance the person from their troublesome behaviour, it is essential that labels or phrases such as 'you're a troublemaker', 'you make me sick' and 'you're a thorough pain in the neck' are avoided. Instead, the focus is always on the behaviour, such as 'this type of behaviour is just not on', 'we really need to work on making sure this behaviour does not happen again'. By criticising the behaviour without the use of personal labels, teachers can convey their effort to maintain a supportive relationship with the pupil, so that the pupil does not feel socially excluded from the school nor that their misbehaviour is an inevitable consequence of who they are.

The role of moral education

A number of writers have argued that a very important way in which schools can combat juvenile delinquency is through moral education. They make the point that many pupils simply do not believe that certain criminal behaviour is unacceptable, and that if schools were able to help instil in pupils stronger moral beliefs and values it would help them resist the temptations to engage in crime. The debate about what pupils think is right and wrong is a confused one. In general, the vast majority of pupils are clear as to what behaviour is right or wrong, at least in so far as knowing what is illegal. Few pupils, for example, would argue that shoplifting is not a crime. What some pupils may argue, however, is that such crimes are acceptable behaviours within the frame of reference that they and their friends are using. Comments such as 'we all do it', 'it's natural' and 'why not?' simply reflect the view that the fact that an act is criminal is not a sufficient deterrent given the personal gains that they may derive from the crime, such as excitement, material rewards and increased esteem in the eyes of their peer group. Consequently moral education needs to focus not so much on conveying that certain crimes are wrong, but on helping pupils to understand that crimes will damage themselves and others, and that any apparent increase in status they think would follow is an illusion and misguided.

Both PSHE and citizenship education provide opportunities to consider pupils' attitudes towards the law, and in particular to involve inputs from outside agencies, such as the police, to discuss how local community projects can help reduce youth crime. During such discussion, pupils occasionally make personal disclosures, either in class or to individual teachers, regarding illegal activity. The guidance on confidentiality produced by the QCA (2000) points out that if a pupil discloses involvement in illegal activity, action should be taken in the best interests of the pupil. This does not necessarily involve informing the police. Teachers are not statutorily required to inform the police about illegal drug activity, for example. The school's police liaison officer will provide guidance about specific instances. Teachers, however, must ensure the pupil is aware of the risks and encourage them to seek support from their parents.

Smith (1999) has looked at the role of moral education in combating juvenile delinquency. He concludes that there is very little evidence that the level of moral reasoning displayed by juvenile delinquents is any different from that of others, and that consequently programmes aimed at improving moral reasoning are unlikely to be an effective strategy in reducing juvenile delinquency. Rather, what is needed is character or values training, in which offenders are encouraged to see crimes as repugnant. For example, victim–offender mediation can have a powerful effect in helping offenders feel more sympathy for victims and become more aware of how their crimes harm others. Offenders are particularly surprised to see the degree of trauma often displayed by the victims of crime. Effective character and values training can also help develop pupils' ability to resist coercion from peers, for example, in experimenting with drugs.

Raising self-esteem

One of the major factors that makes some pupils vulnerable to becoming a juvenile delinquent is low self-esteem. In order to increase a pupil's ability to resist coercion from peers, their own character and self-esteem need to be built up. Some programmes aim to do this by offering such pupils an adult mentor who can act as a role model and help build up the pupil's belief in themselves, particularly if their family circumstances are problematic. Another approach to building up a pupil's self-esteem is to offer them opportunities to be successful in outdoor pursuits, such as learning to sail a large sailing boat, where trust, responsibility, teamwork, perseverance and determination are all needed to achieve success.

Combating persistent offending

As well as including such activities for all pupils in a school, some programmes have been targeted at pupils who are at risk of becoming persistent offenders, and have generally been successful in reducing the incidence of subsequent offending. A typical project involves setting up a panel of representatives from different agencies (teachers, local education authority officers, the police, health workers and social workers) to identify pupils in the local community, usually in the age range of 10 to 14 years, who are at serious risk of turning to crime. This identification process takes into account not just simply persistent misbehaviour at school, but also factors such as living in a high-crime neighbourhood, having a family member involved in crime, or a family history of drugs or child abuse. The intervention programme for such pupils will address a range of problems, and offer personal tuition in numeracy and literacy to help raise the pupils' educational attainment, mentoring, and specialist support to deal with emotional, mental health and drug-related problems. It is interesting to note that when the parents of these pupils are visited at home to see if the parents and the pupil are willing to cooperate with the programme, the vast majority of parents are happy to agree to this. Indeed, most parents indicate they are desperate for such help and support, as many of these pupils will also be causing problems at home for their parents.

Farrington and Welsh (1999) looked at a range of programmes which included some kind of family-based intervention (usually parent training or parent education) and skills training for pupils aimed at reducing delinquency. The programmes typically included elements such as the following:

- skills training for pupils based on small group work on topics such as 'what to do when you are angry' and 'how to react to teasing'
- activities aimed at encouraging pupils to feel a greater social attachment or bond with their parents and with the school
- training parents to use consistent disciplinary techniques

- training teachers in classroom management which encourages pupils to develop desirable behaviours and pro-social methods of problem solving.

Farrington and Welsh reported that most of the interventions were effective in reducing anti-social behaviour and later delinquency.

Hollin *et al.* (2002) have highlighted the need to pay attention to developing delinquents' microskills in social situations. They point out that delinquents often tend to jump to conclusions based on pre-set ideas about a situation rather than look closely at the social cues in front of them (e.g. the other person's body language and eye contact), and that this gives rise to the anti-social behaviour that can underpin becoming a delinquent. Pupils whose social skills can be enhanced will gradually have less need to turn to crime in order to compensate for their feelings of social inadequacy and isolation.

ACTION POINTS

Whole-school policy on promoting good behaviour

The first stage in combating delinquency is the promotion of good behaviour in school. A system of positive expectations coupled with support and praise for good behaviour can play an important role in counteracting negative influences on the pupil. The primary years can be extremely influential here in developing pro-social rather than anti-social behaviour.

Breaking the trajectory

Many persistent offenders have a trajectory which starts with misbehaving in the early years of primary school, continues with involvement in bullying (both as bullies and as victims) and exclusion from school, and ends with juvenile delinquency. Any action that can reduce pupil misbehaviour, bullying, truancy and the risk of being excluded will play an important part in reducing delinquency. Of particular importance is support to help the pupil feel part of and included within the school ethos and community.

Avoiding labelling

In dealing with the misbehaviour of pupils at risk of exclusion or involved in crime, it is important to avoid using personal labels about the individual and to focus instead on the misbehaviour itself. This can help avoid a situation where derogatory personal labels impact on the pupil's self-perceptions and simply encourage further misbehaviour.

Moral education

Moral education deals with the notion of 'the good'. Behaving well in school towards other members of the school community, and considering one's role in society as a good citizen, can enable pupils to avoid being pressured by others into crime. Both PSHE and citizenship education can help promote more positive attitudes towards the law. In particular, role-play activities, videos and outside speakers can help pupils understand the experience of victims of crime, and help undermine the view that those who commit crimes should be admired. Such sessions can also help pupils to consider the personal consequences for them of committing crimes, including the effects of drug addiction, being in prison, and the breakdown of their social relationships.

Drugs education

Much youth crime is simply a means of getting money to fund a drugs habit. Education programmes which combat drug abuse will thereby impact on reducing delinquency.

Improving pupils' emotion control and problem-solving skills

Delinquents often have problems controlling their emotions, and are particularly prone to losing their temper. Help and training in developing socially acceptable methods of conflict resolution, and in how to handle situations where there is a danger of being a bully or being bullied, can be effective in reducing troublesome behaviour.

Home–school communication and cooperation

Parents can be helped to play a key role in encouraging pupils to behave well in school. This can include giving parents advice on their role and on good parenting and the use of appropriate discipline techniques. Once a pupil is identified as being at risk of exclusion or has committed a crime, parents need to be involved in the action taken to support the pupil. For many pupils and their parents involvement with the police can be a shock, and the school can capitalise on the urgency created by this to nip the development of criminal activity in the bud.

Boosting pupils' self-esteem through outdoor pursuits

Pupils at risk of delinquency often have low self-esteem and are particularly vulnerable to being coerced by peers into committing a crime. Any activity that can strengthen a pupil's self-esteem will help combat this. In particular, outdoor pursuits can give certain pupils a real boost.

Involvement in community intervention projects

The school can also play a part in cooperating with a community intervention programme which targets pupils at risk of turning to crime.

Some schemes involve school-based activities during holiday periods, at weekends and in the evening after school, which include personal tuition in literacy and numeracy as well as social and recreational activities.

Mentoring

Pupils at risk of delinquency are often in need of adults who are good role models, particularly if they live in a dysfunctional family. Adults who can act as a mentor can provide a role model and a source of advice and encouragement that the pupils are otherwise lacking in their life.

Exclusion

Whilst it is important to avoid excluding pupils where possible, a fixed-period exclusion can have a positive effect on some pupils in helping them to appreciate the gravity of their situation. It can also help facilitate the involvement of outside agencies which may be able to offer the pupil and their family additional support. Sometimes the misbehaviour that leads to an exclusion is really a form of attention seeking, and in some cases if the pupil is not excluded they may increase their attention-seeking behaviour by turning to crime. Exclusion can therefore sometimes be a force for the good, but this depends on making use of it in a way that empowers the pupil to improve their behaviour.

References

Beinart, S., Anderson, B., Lee, S. and Utting, D. (2002) *Youth at Risk? A National Survey of Risk Factors, Protective Factors and Problem Behaviour among Young People in England, Scotland and Wales.* London: Communities that Care.

Benda, B. B. and Corwyn, R. F. (2000) 'A test of the validity of delinquency syndrome construct in a homogeneous sample.' *Journal of Adolescence*, 23(4), 497–511.

Carroll, A., Baglioni, A. J., Houghton, S. and Bramston, P. (1999) 'At-risk and not at-risk primary school children: an examination of goal orientations and social reputations.' *British Journal of Educational Psychology*, 69(3), 377–92.

Croall, H. (1998) *Crime and Society in Britain.* London: Longman.

Cullingford, C. (1999) *The Causes of Exclusion: Home, School and the Development of Young Criminals.* London: Kogan Page.

Cullingford, C. and Morrison, J. (1995) 'Bullying as a formative influence: the relationship between the experience of school and criminality.' *British Educational Research Journal*, 21(5), 547–60.

Cullingford, C. and Morrison, J. (1997) 'Peer group pressure within and outside school.' *British Educational Research Journal*, 23(1), 61–80.

Farrington, D. P. (1995) 'The development of offending and antisocial behaviour from childhood: key findings from the Cambridge Study in Delinquent Development.' *Journal of Child Psychology and Psychiatry*, 36(6), 929–64.

Farrington, D. P. (1999) 'Predicting persistent young offenders.' In G. L. McDowell and J. S. Smith (eds) *Juvenile Delinquency in the United States and the United Kingdom* (pp. 3–21). London: Sage.

Farrington, D. P. (2000) *Explaining Youth Crime.* London: Wiley.

Farrington, D. P. and Welsh, B. C. (1999) 'Delinquency prevention using family-based interventions.' *Children and Society*, 13(4), 287–303.

Gottfredson, D. C. (2001) *Schools and Delinquency.* Cambridge: Cambridge University Press.

Graham, J. and Bowling, B. (1995) *Young People and Crime (Home Office Research Study 145).* London: Home Office.

Hollin, C. R., Browne, D. and Palmer, E. J. (2002) *Delinquency and Young Offenders.* Oxford: BPS Blackwell.

Johnson, M. J. and Shaw, W. J. (2001) 'Delinquency and criminal behaviour.' In C. E. Walker and M. C. Roberts (eds) *Handbook of Clinical Child Psychology*, 3rd edn (pp. 776–803). Chichester: Wiley.

Mendel, R. A, (2001) *Less Hype, More Help: Reducing Juvenile Crime, What Works – and What Doesn't.* Washington: American Youth Policy Forum.

Moffitt, T. E. (1993) 'Adolescence-limited and life-course-persistent antisocial behaviour: a developmental taxonomy.' *Psychological Review*, 100(4), 674–701.

Moffitt, T. E., Caspi, A., Rutter, M. and Silva, P. A. (2001) *Sex Differences in Anti-Social Behaviour: Conduct Disorder, Delinquency and Violence in the Dunedin Longitudinal Study.* Cambridge: Cambridge University Press.

Muncie, J. (1999) *Youth and Crime: A Critical Introduction.* London: Sage.

QCA (2000) *Citizenship at Key Stages 3 and 4: Initial Guidance for Schools.* London: Qualifications and Curriculum Authority.

Roger, D. (1997) 'Crime and emotion control.' In J. E. Hodge, M. McMurran and C. R. Hollin (eds) *Addicted to Crime?* (pp. 67–85). Chichester: Wiley.

Smith, J. S. (1999) 'Reducing delinquency by improving character.' In G. L. McDowell and J. S. Smith (eds) *Juvenile Delinquency in the United States and the United Kingdom* (pp. 163–82). London: Sage.

Social Exclusion Unit (1998) *Truancy and School Exclusion.* London: The Stationery Office.

Webb, R. and Vulliamy, G. (2002) *The 'Meeting Need and Challenging Crime in Partnership with Schools' Project: An Evaluation, Research Findings No. 162.* London: Home Office Research, Development and Statistics Directorate.

10 Conclusion

There is little doubt that the efforts made to ensure that as far as possible pupils' needs are met within mainstream schools means that new teachers need to be well prepared for their role in helping pupils who face adverse circumstances. In addition, experienced teachers need to know more about the strategies and intervention programme that schools can put in place to help pupils cope with difficult situations they may find themselves in. Moreover, all teachers, both new and experienced, need to be kept well informed about their precise role and duties in dealing with pupils facing problems; this should take account of the legal context that they are working within and the fact that they work within a context of partnership with other teachers, parents, outside agencies and of course the pupils themselves. It is hoped that this book has gone some way to fulfilling this need in presenting an overview of what we know about these adverse circumstances and the role that teachers and schools can play in helping pupils to deal with them.

Index